MIND YOUR LANGUAGE

SEVEN STEPS TO SUCCESS THROUGH WORD POWER

by NICOLA MÉNAGE

Mind Your Language
Seven Steps to Success through Word Power
by

Nicola Ménage

A catalogue record for this book is available from the British Library.
ISBN: 978-0-9927511-0-4

I dedicate this book to my parents,
Alan and Maurean Ménage.

CONTENTS

Introduction

I started to write *Mind Your Language* back in the summer of 2011, when I was given a fabulous opportunity to "dog sit" on the island of Lanzarote. For two weeks I settled down to writing all that I had observed as a therapist, working with clients for the last ten years. I thought about how my work listening to someone's language and helping them to turn around negative and disempowering words and phrases has been both simple and effective. I reflected on how my clients' confidence soared, their perspective changed and problems diminished.

Once back from Lanzarote, I found that life took over once more. Our cosy family life completely changed as first the family dog died and, six months later, my husband and I unexpectedly separated.

Re-reading the book today, I realise that not only has my life significantly altered, I too have changed. My usual character is an enthusiast – upbeat and energetic. What has been illuminating throughout the writing process is that, while going through all the emotions that come with a major life change, my positive language has occasionally slipped. Self-doubt, fear and loss of confidence have taken over – all the old stuff I thought I had dealt with. The interesting experiment for me is that I know that, just by carefully reframing and choosing to swap over my words, stand back and observe, I can and do pull myself back.

The point I am making is that we have enormous capabilities to change and influence our own behaviour. Huge amounts of research, papers and books are published on the power of our brains. Neuroscience and neuro-plasticity are gaining in popularity as we begin to make sense of the awesome influence we have over how we can decide to go through life. The evidence is there that, through our words and thoughts, we can change the pattern of our neurological pathways, influencing our self-determination, motivation, health and outlook on life.

We are all living in changing times that stretch us in many ways. Daily, we are fed bad news about the recession, wars, disease and the decline of the human condition. Yet I fervently believe that we can choose to alter our own perceptions by minding our own language and powering up our words.

This book is for you and will save your life if you are fed up with going through life missing out on promotion and business opportunities or cheesed off with not being heard or continually selling yourself short.

Mind Your Language: Seven Steps to Success through Word Power is a simple book, full of real-life observations, case studies and practical exercises. The exercises at the end of each chapter help to anchor your learning and understanding.

It is simple enough to change your language, although it does mean taking some time to look more closely at yourself, to discover more about the authentic you.

"Life is just too short to live an unhappy existence ... do something about it now. Change your words!"

Is this Book for You?

Over the last decade in my motivational hypnotherapy practice, I have worked successfully with accountants, lawyers, barristers, journalists, broadcasters, actors, writers, restaurant owners, marketers, PR people, doctors, nurses, therapists, teachers, plumbers, electricians, entrepreneurs and so on. These people came to me because they wanted to change how they felt, how they behaved and how they lived their lives. They wanted to have more successful businesses and careers, and to realise their potential. They sought more satisfying relationships, with themselves and with others, and they desired to get more out of life. The majority of these people all shared one thing – how they saw themselves. Interestingly, in every single case their language was limiting and focused on coming from a place of lack. I helped them by showing how using positive Power Up Words can turn their lives around.

This book is for you if you choose:

- To be taken more seriously in your career, to get noticed and get promoted – you will learn how to define who you are and the type of clients and work you want to attract.

- To ensure you are a more effective dynamic leader – you will learn how to speak with more clarity, becoming more motivational and inspirational.

- To drastically improve your financial opportunities and to increase your productivity you will learn how to stop coming from a place of lack and start to come from a position of thinking and speaking with financial authority.

- To cut the constant stream of negativity and improve your personal fulfilment – you will learn how to improve your relationships, increase your sense of self-worth and self-confidence.

- To discover and stay more in touch with your authentic self – you will learn how to find out who you really are and live to your strengths.

- To get out of your rut and move on – you will learn how to change your language and attitude to enhance your vision to live your goals.

- To improve your memory – you will learn how to rely on and trust in your memory.

- To let go of stress – you will learn how to talk yourself into feeling and being calmer and healthier.

Everyone can benefit from learning how to mind your language by powering up their words.

So if you are:

- sceptical and have an open mind

- prepared to look at yourself and change the way you think

Mind Your Language
is for people who
are serious about
improving themselves,
looking to transform
how they think, feel
and see dynamically
and quickly.

- committed and prepared to put in a bit of work

- unhappy as you are, and keen to make beneficial changes,

Welcome! I trust you will benefit from this enjoyable programme to Power Up your life with the clarity of your words. Follow these easy steps and you will start to see benefits in all of the following areas and more:

✓ Your career

✓ Your business

✓ Your finances

✓ Your motivation

✓ Your relationships

✓ Your vision

✓ Your self-confidence

✓ Your memory

Step One:

The Power of Your Mind

The Power of Your Mind

In Step One, we

- **meet the two levels of your mind**

- **explore patterns of behaviour**

- **understand how your mind processes a good or bad word**

- **learn how your language determines your success**

- **discover how you can shape your future**

Meet the Two Levels of Your Mind

Most people, when asked what is their understanding of their subconscious, say something along the lines of "it is responsible for our dreams". That is true; however, it is far more complex. A good starting point is to understand the power of our subconscious mind and how it is fundamental to all of our behaviours.

Our mind is made up of the **conscious** and the **subconscious** (often called your unconscious).

An easy way to understand how the mind works is to think of an iceberg. Above the water is our conscious thought and below the water our subconscious. Approximately 25% of our brain is our conscious mind

Did you know that while your conscious brain is thinking one thought, your non-conscious brain is thinking five thoughts?

and the remaining vast expanse is our subconscious mind.Your conscious brain is the questioning, intellectual rational part of your mind containing your short-term memory. It is able to concentrate on only a limited number of things at one time. It functions mainly as a yes/no computer, constantly analysing, rationalising and discriminating your thoughts.

Our subconscious mind is just like a giant computer; everything we have ever experienced is stored away, like a giant information disc. Our subconscious is responsible for the habit centre, our emotions, creativity, our intuition, long-term memory and self-preservation mechanisms; it also controls all of our bodily functions.

The subconscious mind is in charge of the vast majority of our actions – the things you do without thinking. Consequently, subconscious behaviour and reactions to situations are formed from our strong beliefs and perceptions, and from repetition as well as from social influence.

When people say "But that's the way I've always done it", we know it's simply a habit or pattern of behaviour. Many of our behavioural patterns are useful and those that aren't we can choose to change. The subconscious receives all information as a given; it doesn't have the ability to ask "Does he really mean this?" So when I ask you not to think of a beautiful blue, yellow and turquoise spotted parrot I expect you will be thinking of just that. Why? Because our subconscious has latched onto the creative imagery of the parrot, and disregarded the word "not".

The simplest way to explain how our subconscious works is to see its function as a giant computer. It absorbs everything we have ever experienced, such as emotions, thoughts, experiences. A significant part of our subconscious mind is the capacity we have as human beings to play back experiences just like retelling stories. So that last cigarette, or last glass of wine, for example, was fantastic, although in reality it was just like any other cigarette; as time elapses, our memory recall for storytelling becomes stronger and stronger. Every time we recount an experience or a feeling we reinforce the story.

So for example the statement, "I just can't seem to get a promotion, I always miss out, I'm just not good enough" or "I'm absolutely useless at public speaking, I get embarrassed and tongue tied" starts off in the brain as a little neuro signal, a trickle, like a small stream, and the more we repeat it, the stronger and stronger and the more and more believable it becomes to ourselves, until it ends up like a torrential river pouring forth its reinforcing message, until we have established our own believable, unshakeable schema. We have created our own new story.

The subconscious takes everything at face value and is unable to differentiate between fact and fiction. We create our very own blueprint. This book sets out to demonstrate simply how we can help to alter our master blueprint through choosing our words to change how we behave.

For the many clients I have worked with, I have found the most powerful

Did you know that your conscious brain controls only 2–4% of your behaviour and perception? Whereas your non-conscious brain controls a huge 96–98% of your behaviour and perception!

and efficient way to change deep-seated unwanted behaviour and habits is by them making a conscious decision to change their language. The invaluable tools of hypnosis and NLP (Neuro-Linguistic Programming) have assisted with this.

This statistic is even more alarming if you consider Einstein once observed that, for every negative message the brain receives, it takes eleven or more positive messages to negate its effect. When we consider we live in a world dominated by the "News" (have you noticed how good news rarely makes the News?), it is less easy for children and emerging adults to have confidence, self-esteem and self-worth, and to feel happy.

How the Mind Processes a Positive or a Negative Thought or Word

How the brain works is a complicated topic, and it is still not fully understood. Here is my favourite simple explanation of how our mind processes a positive thought or word. In his book *Goal Mapping* Brian Mayne says:

> *"I learned that everyone has billions of brain cells with 'arms'*
> *called dendrites. (I imagine them to look like a tiny pin prick*
> *with spidery arms and legs.) Each of the dendrites is separated by*
> *a slight gap known as the 'synaptic gap'. When you have a*
> *thought, you spark an impulse in the centre (the nucleus) of the*
> *brain cell that travels along each of the dendrites, seeking to*
> *make connection with other dendrites, so that the thought*

*spreads outwards to form a pattern of understanding, or train
of thought. If your thought is positive – whether to do with
your self, your life, or situation – the positive impulse triggers
the release of a chemical called 'serotonin' from the end of the
dendrite 'arm'.*

*Serotonin is the chemical that gives you that feeling of happiness
and well-being; it also acts as a conductor and bridges the
synaptic gap, allowing our thought to continue on its journey.
If however the thought you have is negative, it triggers the release
of a chemical called 'cortisol' instead, which prompts feelings of
sadness and depression. It also works as an insulator, effectively blocking
or limiting the free-flow of thoughts and ideas."*

(Goal-Mapping, Brian Mayne)

To clarify, when we use empowering progressive words – let's call them Power Up Words – our brain releases serotonin, creating brain cell connections that help us to reinforce the belief we are achieving, self-determined, happy individuals. In contrast, using a limiting or negative word (a Power Sap Word), or expressing a disempowering word (a Power Cut Word), releases cortisone that helps keep us stuck in how we see ourselves or others see us.

How Our Thoughts and Language Determine Our Success

Throughout life we observe from history and through our experience that success is not a God-given gift, dependent on chance or accident. Yes, some people are born with a silver spoon in their mouth. However, being born into an affluent family doesn't guarantee long-lasting happiness, fulfilment and success; what is crucial for being able to achieve and maintain success is how people think and behave.

True lasting success is not accidental. The pages of numerous books are filled with the names of people who either had a difficult start in life, or failed numerous times before they went on to master the skill of success and achieve unimaginable greatness: Nelson Mandela, Thomas Edison, Jessie Jackson, Oprah Winphrey, Mo Farah, John Lennon and Henry Ford, to name a few examples.

Throughout history, successful people have been studied in order to identify the "habits" of success. The conclusion, surprise, surprise, is that successful people think and speak successful thoughts and words and have a deep-seated belief that they will succeed. They are resourceful and keep on going.

Living in a physical world of cause and effect where what we do produces specific results, every action we take is first triggered by a thought. The main difference between successful people and unsuccessful people is they focus their thoughts, words and phrases on what they want in life, rather than on what they fear, what they don't want.

Successful people create their circumstances by the thoughts they think and the words they speak. And so it follows that unsuccessful people also create their circumstances by their thoughts and words.

For example, when we say a phrase like "Life's so hard", as many people do, it starts a process that changes the thought, first into our behaviour, and then eventually into our circumstances. The result is that life indeed "becomes" difficult, through our perception and our experience. A more uplifting statement, such as "Life is good", also starts a process of change – one that makes us feel better, more optimistic and forward thinking.

Prolific American author, Dr Shad Helmstetter, states in his book, *What to Say When You Talk to Yourself*, that by the time a person reaches the age of 18, they will have heard the word "no" on average a total of 118,000 times from parents or adults in positions of influence or control. In contrast, can you imagine how it would feel to have heard 118,000 "yeses" instead! (However, to say "no" sometimes can be good, and we look at the benefits of being able to say "no" in a positive way in Stage Five.)

The notion of success varies from individual to individual; it may be having a successful thriving business, multiple businesses, rewarding relationships, a family, a nice house, holidays or it may mean living a peaceful harmonious life.

Whilst our thought processes are the same for both the successful and unsuccessful person, their results depend on what each person chooses to focus upon. We all have the ability to choose how to express what we think. Generally I have noticed that successful people choose to express themselves with thoughts and phrases of abundance and opportunity. They work on themselves and never quit! Whilst the "overnight wonders" can become arrogant and quickly disappear, truly successful people work on their personality, their leadership skills, management skills and every other detail of life. When a relationship or business deal goes sour, they assume they can learn from it and they expect to do better next time. Successful people don't tolerate flaws in themselves; they learn to remedy them!

It can be observed that some unsuccessful people focus on lack and limitation; they choose to see life as difficult and a burden, reinforcing the message "No one ever said life would be easy."

Introducing the Law of Sympathetic Resonance

In the 1600s, Christian Huygens invented the pendulum clock. He displayed his clocks on the walls of a room, where each pendulum swung independently. Huygens discovered that, after a while, all the pendulums began to swing in a precise, synchronised rhythm. He theorised that the clocks' sound waves entered the walls, which responded with their own vibrations, thereby bringing the clocks into a single rhythm. Huygens' theory is now a well-accepted law of physics, known as "sympathetic resonance".

Imagine a large ballroom, in one corner of which is a grand piano; striking a tuning fork on one side of the room will cause a piano string on the other side of the room to spontaneously begin to vibrate, sounding either the same note or a harmonic of the note sounded by the tuning fork. This is a principle musicians know well and apply daily, reflecting the Law of Sympathetic Resonance.

The Law of Sympathetic Resonance is also known as the Law of Attraction, or we may refer to it as synchronicity. We are all familiar with what we call a coincidence; for example, thinking of someone we haven't heard of for ages, or someone whom we want to talk to. Then, "Bingo!", literally out of the blue, that person calls you up or you bump into them. Is this a coincidence or is it the Law of Sympathetic Resonance? Quite simply, we are like magnets – what we ask for comes to us – which, fundamentally, is why we have to be aware of the language we use.

You tend to get what you ask for.

A good friend of mine who had experienced a catalogue of challenges all in the same year, including leaving full-time employment to set up her own practice, separating from her husband, selling her house and embarking on a new all-consuming relationship, was getting prepared to go skiing in the Alps. Just before she left she said, "Nicola, I just want a break."

And that is exactly what she got ... she broke her leg in three places, it was pinned and she was immobile for the next three months.

Warning: Be careful what you ask for!

EXERCISE: Being Clear About What You Desire

When you are looking to park your car, visualise a parking spot, even if you are not familiar with where you are. Drive into the car park or street and visualise a lovely space. If there isn't one, drive around once more; you will find, without fail, a space becomes available. Or, if you know where you want to park, drive straight into the space that is waiting for you. Try it!

In Step One you have learned:

- **the difference between our conscious and subconscious mind**

- **how deep ingrained habits are formed**

- **how our mind processes a positive or a negative word**

- **why and how our language determines our success**

- **how what you ask for comes to you**

Points to Focus on

- Surround yourself with the books and audios of positive, successful people. Be aware of the shared characteristics in their behaviour.

- Practise the Law of Sympathetic Resonance and put your attention on something like a car parking space with quiet confidence. Remember the Law doesn't work if you come from a place of desperation.

Step Two:

Finding Your Authentic Self

In Step Two you will

- **establish how what you think and say reinforces how you feel and see yourself**

- **learn how to juice up your subconscious**

- **see why it is important to be authentic**

- **discover your authentic self**

Have you ever wondered why when we hear a piece of music, or smell an old familiar smell, old feelings and memories of a past or long-forgotten event are evoked? If you remember, in Step One we established the important role of the subconscious. Remember, your subconscious takes everything as a given, and retains everything just like a giant sponge, or a large computer. The language of the subconscious is imagery and metaphor. That's why you remember things clearly when your senses are stimulated by smell, stories, films or music.

So, for example, if I say to you "Don't think about a strawberry cream pavlova, topped off with shavings of dark chocolate," I can put money on it that what you are probably thinking of is a strawberry pavlova. Why? Because the imagination loves metaphor and imagery, it focuses on the words that excite it most; probably all your subconscious can see is a strawberry pavlova with cream and chocolate. You may even begin to experience saliva producing in your mouth, with feelings of expectation.

Your subconscious responds to the emotional and the creative. Think about adverts that have had a strong influence on you in the past. Is it the music, the song lyrics or the catchphrase, or perhaps the overall atmosphere you remember? What feelings have they left you with?

The majority of us have the ability to use all of our five senses:

1. Sight

2. Sound

3. Touch

4. Taste

5. Smell

As individuals, we tend to be slightly more predisposed to one sense more than the others; either visual, kinaesthetic (meaning taste, touch and smell) or auditory. You may find you have a strong use of three or more of your senses. Therefore you respond more to language that appeals to your senses. In Step Two, you will explore your senses further.

"Two trends govern our current world; that is to create an emotional response in our target audience and to be credible and true."

(Joel Roberts, media coach and former KABC prime-time radio presenter, Los Angeles)

When you hear someone give a speech, what is it you remember weeks or even years later? Very little of the actual information is retained; it is the overall impression, the feeling, the emotion that person left you with. It is their words and tone of voice that creates a feeling about them, and an emotion of indifference, dislike or excitement that you recall.

Therefore it is essential that the words you do use are clear, concise, colourful and emotive, to juice up your subconscious. Excitement will inspire dynamic action, leaving a lasting impression on yourself and others.

The Language of the Subconscious is Imagery and Metaphor

Would you agree with me that people do business with people they feel confident with and believe in? Yes? Good. This is why the importance of being authentic is crucial. When you deny living your truth, living who you are, you are sending out a clear message to your customers that you lack belief in yourself, your product, your business. People want to feel safe and secure, and they want to know they can trust you to deliver.

A good illustration is Del Boy, the character played by David Jason in the popular long-running television series *Only Fools and Horses* in the 1980s and 1990s. Although a loveable character, he had us cringing at the same time. In later episodes, in the spirit of Thatcher's Britain, determined to better himself, Del Boy adopted the practice of "faking it till you make it". He thought he could do this by showing off his then much desired Filofax, wearing suits, a Barbour trench coat and carrying a silver metallic briefcase. He drank in the up and coming wine bars of Peckham, giving the "city boys and girls" the impression he was a market trader, failing to mention he was referring to Peckham market rather than the Stock Exchange!

Del Boy was neither convincing, nor authentic, despised by the city folk, never quite clinching that golden nugget of a deal. He also alienated his long-term friends back in his local pub, because his language and behaviour was lacking authenticity. He was incongruent, ridiculed by all for being a fake. Being false didn't work – what worked for Del Boy was being honestly dishonest!

Changing your words to what makes you feel comfortable, confident and motivated gives a clear message to your customers, colleagues and others that you are believable and trustworthy and in safe hands.

A beneficial example of this was when Labour leader Gordon Brown, in his summing up of the 2010 televised election debates in the run up to the general election, declared he was "desperate to govern the people for the next term". Clearly, Gordon coming from a place of desperation didn't swing it for the nation as his party lost to a coalition government.

In contrast, here is an extract from President Obama's inaugural speech back in January 2009:

"We remain a young nation, but in the words of Scripture, the time has come to set aside childish things. The time has come to reaffirm our enduring spirit; to choose our better history; from generation to generation: the God-given promise that all are equal, all are free, and all deserve a chance to pursue their full measure of happiness. For everywhere we look, there is work to be done ...
The state of our economy calls for action: bold and swift. And we will act not only to create new jobs but to lay a new foundation for growth.
We will build the roads and bridges, the electric grids and digital lines that feed our commerce and bind us together.
We will restore science to its rightful place and wield technology's wonders to raise health care's quality."

At the time Obama's delivery and well-chosen words were received as inspiring, motivational and confident; the world was left with little doubt that Obama was the right man to head up the United States of America during those radically changing economic times.

The key theme that came across about Obama is that his message was congruent. We knew he believed in himself; that he was confident and self-assured, and renowned for his use of pure oratory. In his speech, he used wonderful emotive words like action, bold and swift, build, bridges, feed, bind, restore, reaffirm, wonders, raise, care, quality. It was a speech coming from knowledge and from the heart.

Furthermore, for the majority at the time of delivery he was believable, convincing and passionate, he spoke his truth, was authentic, and we believed him. Eric Heath from Stanford University commented:

"To listen to an adult speaking to adults: What a refreshing change. To hear a call to our generosity of spirit: It is a new day indeed."

The same can be true about Sir Winston Churchill's speeches; he also used oratory. Whatever our opinion of these two leaders, we all remember how they made us feel.

Your Authentic Self

How I Discovered My Authentic Self

We quite often hear the statements bandied around, "Be true to yourself", or "Be your authentic self" or "Live your truth". I want to share a significant experience that influenced who I am today, which illustrates the meaning of these statements.

About twelve years ago I took my two daughters to see their favourite children's author Jacqueline Wilson at Chipping Norton Theatre. It was a Saturday morning and as we approached the theatre, the long queue, comprising children and adults, snaked around the corner.

We took our seats in the balcony; the atmosphere was one of excitement and anticipation. Then out she stepped onto the stage … instantly, there was a hush. Before us was a small, slim, short white-haired lady in her early 60s, dressed in black, looking trendy and rather gothic. She wore little round glasses and on each finger she wore large silver rings.

She captured the audience and held our attention for over an hour and a half. She was spellbinding. Every child and many adults too were her raving fans. We hung on her every word. We were there because we loved her books; they were funny, sad, they touched on the raw harsh facts of life from a child's perspective. Divorce, alcoholism, fostering and more, yet we couldn't get enough of them or her. And at one point I became overwhelmed with emotion, tears flowing down my cheeks.

So what was it that had touched me?

It was her enthusiasm, her passion. It felt like she was talking to us in her sitting room. She was so natural, so at home with a large audience; she was compassionate, and above all respectful. I felt touched by her sensitivity. She was professional to her finger tips, funny, brave, poignant.

The reason for my tears was that she touched a part of me … a part of me that knew I wasn't being true to myself, I wasn't living my true purpose, I wasn't in touch with my creative self, nor was I feeling fulfilled.

As a child in primary school about the age of seven I was allowed periodically to stay inside at lunchtimes with a small band of others. In those lunchtimes we went to the hall and, using the box of dressing-up clothes and a few props, we would put on a play for the rest of the school. I was usually the director, writer and producer. I can only imagine how bossy and unbearable I must have been!

Somewhere along the way I lost my confidence; in my senior school I would be full of admiration for the girls acting in the school plays, never daring to put myself forward for auditions, and feeling decidedly not good enough.

A couple of years after the Jacqueline Wilson experience I discovered what my purpose was and that is why today I work as a motivational hypnotherapist. My purpose is to:

- assist men and women who want to make exciting changes to their lives

- help them discover how to live their truth

- feel happier, more in control and live the life they want

- help bring joy and fulfilment and improved health

I love my work and gain huge pleasure and satisfaction working with those who can discover who they are, free from their own limitations.

For the last two years I have taken to the bigger stage and experience a great buzz and rush of pleasure when I am speaking in public. At long last I am being true to myself, performing and sharing my message to others. So thank you Jacqueline Wilson for helping to show me how to live my truth.

The Phenomenal Power of Your Subconscious Mind

The subconscious is powerful. Here's an example from my case files.

CASE STUDY

All his life, Paul felt he wasn't good enough for the job, working as a marketing executive for a big high street retailer. He recounted to me that he had worked for the company for the last ten years and believed he was still there only by the skin of his teeth. He saw himself as a fraud, and felt he was close to being discovered as the wrong man for the job.

Paul came to me as a client because he felt there was something missing. Straight away I picked up on his body language, his words and also his tone of voice.

Paul came from a place of lack; a bachelor, he craved a long-term partner and to feel included. He said he always felt he was on the periphery of life.

He lacked confidence and held a deep-rooted self-belief that he was worthless, a nobody. So much so that he took Valium to calm his nerves when he attended board meetings and gave presentations.

Smart and meticulous about his appearance, Paul was tall but sat curled up with his arms and legs crossed, head and shoulders bowed. His voice would tail off weakly when he had something to say. He lacked charisma and presence. In short, he was a walking apology.

As he began to relax, I picked up that when he became motivated about something he would become very articulate and funny. Part of Paul's problem was he gave his power away by the language he used; he apologised for expressing an opinion and peppered his conversation with "sorry", "try", "need" and "should". He responded to what he thought people wanted to hear. Because he felt worthless, he responded with disempowering language. He gave his power away to colleagues and in relationships, trying to please and to do what he thought was the right thing.

After just four sessions together, we managed to turn Paul's life around. After the first session I asked him to get six work colleagues and friends whom he trusted to write down and seal in an envelope exactly what they thought were Paul's main strengths and weaknesses.

The following session, he opened up the envelopes rather tentatively. My hunch was right – they all considered Paul to be an intelligent, witty guy who didn't believe in himself, a follower rather than a leader.

We set to work on unravelling his negative self-belief; part of the fundamental work was to change the negative language he used. The speed at which he changed his life around was phenomenal. After each subsequent session he came back to report major steps forward. As he began to feel more confident, he lost his hunched-up appearance and adopted a pleasing middle tone of voice, projecting yet more confidence.

And, happily there's more:

- He dramatically changed his language by using progressive words, eradicating apologies and limiting words.

- He stopped telling people what he thought they wanted to hear; he started to come from a place of keeping his power.

- He stopped taking Valium before board meetings and giving presentations. The result was that people began to embrace his straight talking and his sense of humour.

- He was asked to lead the team away-day, a coveted position that traditionally suggested you were on your way up.

- He asked out a lady he had had his eye on for several months and began a new and fulfilling relationship.

Once you know yourself better, you can make more authentic choices.

EXERCISE: Discovering Your Strengths and Weaknesses

Ask five or six people you know and trust – work colleagues, friends and family – what they see as your main qualities and weaknesses.

Discovering the Real Authentic You

EXERCISE: The Characteristics of Trust

One

Fold a blank piece of paper in half length-wise or draw a line down the middle.

Two

Open the paper and on the left hand side write down the names of six people you trust.

Three

On the right hand column jot down what characteristics you admire about each person. This is a quick exercise – aim to take no longer than five minutes to complete.

Once you have completed the exercise, consider what unites all of the people you have mentioned.

Do they share the same characteristics? If so, which are they? What do you admire about them that you feel is lacking in yourself?

Take the message and begin to incorporate their qualities into your life.

For example, when I first did this exercise I was struck how all the people I had on my list were 100% reliable and good at their jobs. They always delivered on time and with an excellent service; they were discreet, willing and friendly. It reinforced those characteristics I strove to deliver in all aspects of my life. Again, remember that like attracts like.

EXERCISE: Find and Live Your Authentic Self

On a blank piece of paper write the following statement:

"My natural given talents are:"

Close your eyes and focus on your breath for a bit; just take some time to be aware of yourself. If your attention wanders bring it back to your breath.

After several minutes say the statement out loud "My natural given talents are …" Then cast your mind back to your early years. To assist the process you may like to recall the primary school you went to. Imagine the classroom, the playground, the house where you grew up. Recall as best you can details, sounds and other sensations.

What was it you were naturally good at? What did your teachers, parents, significant adults say positively about you? Immediately write down the answers that come to you.

Are you incorporating your natural early talents into your life now … today?

Recap

When you use empowering words that Power Up your subconscious, you will instantly feel more confident and in control.

Keep your power, use positive words, drop limiting negative words that send a message to yourself that you are a worthless, desperate individual.

Be who you are, rather than how you think other people want you to be. The more you live a lie, the more unbelievable and lacking in confidence you become. Be authentic ... live your truth and enjoy being you.

In Step Two you have learned:

- **how to juice up your subconscious to get what you want**

- **the importance of being authentic**

- **how to find your authentic self**

- **to value yourself**

Time to Focus

- Write down your strengths, characteristics and what you think about yourself.

- Start to live your authentic self – think about how you can incorporate your natural early talents into your future life.

- Think about how you can reinforce your own trust characteristics.

Step Three:

Harnessing the Power of Your Mind

Harnessing the Power of Your Mind

In Stage Three you will:

- **make friends with your Subby**

- **understand where negative thoughts come from**

- **learn to control your negative thoughts**

- **differentiate between keeping your power vs. giving your power away**

Make Friends with Your Subby

Before we go any further, it is about time I introduced you to your Subby. Subby is your friend, your amigo – someone or something that will never let you down. Develop a healthy relationship with your Subby and it will always be there with and for you, through sickness and health, the good and not so good times – in fact, throughout the rest of your life.

A talented Australian hypnotherapist, the late Mervin Minall-Jones, passed on the Subby legacy and I want to pass it on to you. Mervin coined the term "Subby" when he referred to his subconscious.

My Subby is with me now constantly as my friend and advisor. Some people may refer to it as the gremlin or the nagging internal voice. Believe me, once you get to know and work with your Subby you can quieten the inner critic and really start to enjoy life.

Why Making Friends with Your Subby is Good for Your Success

When a small child begins to start its first adventurous tottering walks, those initial steps are tentative, wobbly, uncertain. What do we do when they fall down, as of course they will? Do we tell them off and tell them they're useless, idiots, and not to bother to try walking as it's a waste of time? Or do we pick them up, brush them down, give them a hug and give them encouragement. I think you'll agree the latter is largely what we do – we nurture, encourage and care for them, we want them to succeed. And generally they do succeed. They go on to walk, skip, jump and run, and they embrace life to its fullest; they have a world to explore and to conquer.

The crucial point I want to make here is that when you constantly allow your imaginary gremlin, your internal critic, to take over, to continually beat you with negative disempowering language and thoughts, the impact is destructive and limits your potential, your vision and your impact.

When your subconscious has a continual barrage of put-downs from you, it clams up, it becomes nervous and unconfident; it actually becomes dysfunctional. For example, if you continually remind yourself you are old, ugly, unattractive, useless, forgetful, thick and stupid, that is exactly how you will look, act and behave.

CASE STUDY

James was a businessman and for some time had been experiencing a crisis of confidence. Periodically, as part of his job, he was required to chair a large trade association.

James was locked in a destructive, negative belief pattern. He was experiencing poor sleep, was anxious and his confidence was at a low point. He came to see me as he had reached breaking point. In a few weeks' time he had another meeting coming up where he was due to give a keynote speech.

After initial discussions I quickly realised he had suffered an unfortunate experience at a talk he had given over a year ago. He had been unwell, and his resulting speech was lacking polish and some key details. Ever since, he had beaten himself up, telling himself he was useless and an idiot and a failure.

To reframe the negative experience, I planted a strong hypnotic programme, suggesting to James how confident he felt, how relaxed and prepared he was, and how well he knew his material. Under hypnosis, he saw himself standing tall in full flow, loud and clear, and engaging with the audience. An essential element of this work was to introduce James to his Subby. At the end of our session I asked him to give me a call to let me know how the talk had gone.

Several days later, he called to say how pleased he was. James had told himself, as he was waiting to go on to speak, "It's alright, James, because I'm here, we can support each other." This result, as you can imagine, was music to my ears!

Before qualifying as a hypnotherapist and studying the power of our subconscious I was extremely forgetful, always forgetting my keys and important information, making numerous lists and so on. Having developed my unique, trusting relationship with my Subby, I know I can rely on my subconscious, and the more relaxed it is the better it performs for me. It always delivers – I rarely make lists now. This is because we are working in harmony together, we have a trusting, lasting relationship and we are in it together for the long haul. My Subby can relax. When the name of someone or something escapes me, I say to myself, it will come, I know the name, it will come in a minute, and, "Bingo!", it does come. I have stopped worrying; I know that I will remember. As a result my Subby relaxes and, because it feels relaxed, it stops blocking that thought process and the temporary perceived forgotten fact or name just pops up. Trust me, it never fails.

When people tell me flippantly they have early onset Alzheimer's, or are experiencing a senior moment (and they are only in their mid-40s), they think they're being wry.

What they clearly are unable to see is they are reinforcing their subconscious, giving it permission to be forgetful, to age quicker. Remember, Subby thinks "Yes, that is my instruction," so it behaves just like it is told. People expect their memory to perform at its optimum; however, when they constantly tell themselves they are having a senior moment, or they mustn't forget, that's exactly what happens – they forget. It is a reinforcement.

This brings to mind the case of Jenny whom I worked with several years ago.

CASE STUDY

Jenny had suffered a dual trauma at work and in her personal life, resulting in her having prolonged bouts of memory loss and a complete "shutting down", as she termed it. As a result, she went through life on tiptoes in order to avoid upsetting people. Her behaviour was particularly impaired when she was put under pressure in new situations; hence, her professional and personal life were severely impacted.

She wrote, "I feel I have lost my identity, my value as a person. Then as you witnessed I meet complete blankness, I feel nothing, I can't communicate and generally feel like a failure across the board with every aspect in my life. I feel stupid, I can't remember anything. I get so cross with myself … this 'shut down' is stimulated by panic and self-doubt. I just become nothing as a person … and berate myself, coming across like a blithering idiot."

The work to do in this case was to reinforce to her Subby that she can relax in perceived difficult situations, to change her language from negative limiting words.

A great trick is to be able to stand back and acknowledge when our negative ego voice comes up. At first it is a little whisper, and as we pay more attention to it, its destructive message gets louder and louder until it roars in our ears that we are useless, stupid and not good enough.

TECHNIQUE: SODA

I picked up this technique from a seminar given by Deepak Chopra, a prolific author, metaphysicist and physician. The SODA technique works in the following way and can be applied when we start to feel uncomfortable in a given situation, for example, in relationships, at work or stress-related issues. To avoid reacting and going into ego mode it is beneficial to sit in the "uncomfortable" before you start to feel more comfortable. To get to feeling in a better place, apply the following technique:

S – stop

O – observe what is happening

D – detach emotionally from the situation

A – and then you can move forward...take action, coming from a more controlled place.

When we enter into ego mode, we can give away our power, and we lose control to our ego. Ego is reactive; when we apply SODA we give ourselves the time to calm down and see the situation for what it really is. The ego grows when we give it power and shrinks when it is observed. By acknowledging when the ego is active, we are more able to take back control.

Keeping Your Power versus Giving It Away

Our ego starts to form around about the age of four; it is when we start to become more self-aware and self-conscious of ourselves and others. I am particularly interested in how the negative side of our ego determines how we feel about ourselves, and impacts on our behaviour.

When we are young our ego, which is part of our subconscious, takes on the following typical negative beliefs: fear, insecurity, feelings of lack, inadequacy, jealousy, denial, lack of responsibility, feeling not good enough, apologetic and intolerant, full of anger, hate and self-doubt. You may have some of your own to add to the list. These beliefs and attitudes can be inherited from our parents and teachers, reinforced by early experiences, and stay with us right into adulthood, impacting on our confidence and self-belief. When we are under pressure we can easily slip into negative ego mode, the conscious sense of who we are which is our irrational self and takes over our rational behaviour. What this means is that as adults we revert to child mode, coming from the child-based ego, rather than the grown-up one.

EXERCISE: Your Negative Beliefs

Make a list of ego-driven negative feelings you have about yourself, e.g. fear, jealousy, greed, etc. Then make a parallel,positive list, turning each feeling around, for example, fear becomes courage.

Giving your power away may well be a term familiar to you. The dictionary definition of "power" is the ability to have strength and influence with a capacity to drive something forward. However, the word "power" can, for some people, hold some negative connotations. In this context I want us to explore exactly what I mean and why it is essential to convey through our words that we keep our power.

A self-assured individual who is in control attracts like-minded people like a magnet. (Again, bear in mind the Law of Sympathetic Resonance in Stage One.) Such people are filled with positive energy and come from a place of self-respect. In essence, they are coming from a place of self-power.

Observe their language carefully – they use strong empowering words such as aim, focus, remember, understand, deliver, trust. If they are in the wrong they apologise with sincerity; they are mindful of the misuse of the word "sorry".

In comparison, a person who inadvertently gives their power away comes from a place of blame, victim, lack and fear. Frequent words they use are sorry, try, need, should, could, would, can't, forget, hope, afraid, shame. We focus on these words in closer detail in Stage Four.

TECHNIQUE: Self-talk

Natasha, a good friend of mine and former co-director of the Stratford Literary Festival, passed on this valuable technique. Once the festival starts, there is little breathing space and it is a juggling act to bring everything and everyone together to make this great festival so successful. She recalled how, during the final few days and on her knees with exhaustion, adrenalin, long days and late nights, she practises the following technique.

"As I get in the car to drive the twelve miles into Stratford, feeling exhausted and burnt out from the night before, I start my self-talk. At first it begins with a mutter, barely a whisper, because I can only just sum up the energy.

'I am the lovely Natasha, I am wise, I am witty, I am strong, I am resourceful, I am resilient.' By the time I get into the centre of Stratford, I am in full swing, roaring with great gusto, 'I am terrific, I am talented, I am happy, I am full of energy.' Heaven knows what other people think, but who cares? People probably think I am on my mobile phone."

She says this technique of talking to her Subby never fails, and sustains her until the next day.

Although this is a light-hearted example, if we recall how the brain works, every positive thought Natasha expressed sent new links from each dendrite along its arms, creating and reinforcing a positive message, which in turn released the feel-good chemical serotonin.

What you believe and what you say to yourself have a tremendous impact on what happens to you and what kind of life you lead.

Keeping Your Power

Throughout the book I refer to keeping your power. What this means is coming from a place of the grown-up rather than child-based ego. It is about taking responsibility for our own actions and decisions. It is about completely liking and loving ourselves, no longer blaming anyone else.

When we come from the positioning of

- unconditional love of self,

- respect of self,

- honour of self, and

- acceptance of self,

it is so much easier to use language that fits with how we perceive ourselves as mature grown-ups, rather than as adults who apply reactive child-like behaviour, giving in to the ego.

We all at some time will give our power away, and our ego will begin to whisper and subsequently roar; however, the trick is to see it coming, observe and not feed it … not to give it power. The SODA technique (see earlier in this Step) helps achieve this perfectly.

CASE STUDY

A clear example of this is in the case of 45-year-old IT programme writer, Alan, who came to me for some sessions to help him resolve his crippling self-esteem issues, which periodically reduced him to feeling and reacting like a seven-year-old.

A big contract had failed to meet the client's deadline, due to a number of significant factors outside Alan's control, subsequently costing his company several thousand pounds in lost revenue. His client had called him incompetent, inept and unprofessional. This resulted in Alan developing overwhelming feelings of despair, failure and lack of belief in his own capabilities.

In fact, Alan had lost sight of the fact that this was the first time in 25 years of business that he had failed to deliver on time to a client, and allowed his child-like ego to step in and roar he was useless, stupid and a failure. Although successful in his career, Alan had struggled with low esteem issues throughout his life. His relationship with his father had been fraught with tension, leaving him feeling not good enough, and becoming a non achiever.

Part of our work was to enable Alan to use the SODA technique (see earlier in Step Three), stand back and, through hypnotherapy, reposition his viewpoint as a grown up, i.e. to have self-respect, unconditional love, self-belief and forgiveness.

It is important to remember that whatever we give our attention to grows in strength.

In Step Three you have learned:

- **the effect of negative thoughts on your confidence and memory**

- **the role of the ego**

- **the SODA technique for defusing the ego mode**

- **the importance of retaining your power**

Points to Focus On

Look again at the list of ego-driven negative feelings you have about yourself and consider what value or purpose they offer. Question whether these negative feelings are still relevant to you.

Develop your awareness of SODA and practise it in relevant situations. Witness when your child ego starts to come in and apply SODA to get into a stronger grown-up position.

Step Four:

Power Cut and Power Sap Words to Avoid

Power Cut and Power Sap Words to Avoid

In Step Four you will

- **discover Power Cut Words**

  and

- **explore Power Sap Words**

The English language is renowned for being beautiful as well as complex. The purpose of this book is not to look at the English language and all its inconsistencies; rather, it is intended to help you fine-tune your language so you give a positive and memorable lasting impression.

In Step Four, we look at words that evoke negative feelings, those words that dominate our everyday language. Words and phrases flow from our mouths and we frequently fail to see, hear and feel the impact they have on our subconscious thought, impacting on our energy, our motivation and how others perceive us.

My intention here is to raise your awareness of some of the more common everyday terms that are seriously holding you back and to be mindful of the impression you convey by the words you use. By eradicating these words from your vocabulary, you will feel and be more successful, and feel focused, lighter, happier and, ultimately, more fulfilled.

Power Cut Words

Coming up is a list of frequently used disempowering words that cut your power, which you have inherited along the way. All these words:

- are limiting, restrictive or disempowering

- elicit uncomfortable and negative feelings

- infer subliminally that we come from a place of lack

You will clearly hear the negative message they convey of how we see and feel about ourselves.

My top Power Cut Words are:

Sorry

The national obsession for the most inappropriate word has to be the word "sorry". When we look at the word sorry in the English dictionary it defines "sorry" to mean: apologetic, miserable, pitiful, regretful, remorseful, repentant, sad, sorrowful, unhappy and wretched.

It is a much overused word and I have personally overused the word myself quite inappropriately in the past, because I was brought up within a polite family where we were taught to say sorry a lot. It was considered to be good manners, considerate to others. When I worked with an American trainer back in the late 1990s, he pointed out to me that the British are such a polite nation and frequently feel the need to say sorry. When you look at the definition of the word, it is laughable; we say sorry for everything: "sorry, can you move over please", "sorry to disturb you, sorry can you pass the salt?"

We are even sorry if someone bumps into us – it has become a habit word.

The real use of the word is one of gravitas, to be saved for a serious moment. "I am sincerely sorry to hear about the death of your mother." So please save it for the appropriate occasion.

Once you become more conscious of the words you use, you will be aware of the misuse of the word and its true meaning. If you consider we can use the word "sorry" every five minutes or so, that amounts to a lot of sorrow in people's lives.

By the frequent misuse of the word we continually reinforce to our subconscious that we are sorrowful, apologetic, sad, miserable – literally, a walking apology.

When I stopped overusing the word, it felt so liberating to change my habitual "sorry" and to find more appropriate alternatives. When I do use "sorry", it has much more power to it than just another "sorry" trotted out.

A walking apology

When I was buying my first new car, the car salesman went out of his way to be accommodating, so pleased was he to get a sale. So much so that when it came to arranging the finance details, he continually apologised. Peppering every sentence with a "sorry". Apologising for every little thing, the date of delivery, the terms and conditions, the coffee, the seat I was sitting on, the heat of the sun. He was literally a walking apology; it became quite laughable. My lasting impression of him is of a fraught little man, coming from a place of lack. I was tempted to cancel my sale and take my business elsewhere.

Shame

Shame is another example of a misused word.

"It's a shame it rained on the day of the Queen's Jubilee."

There is no shame; it is simply unfortunate, the luck of the draw. The definition of shame is that it describes a negative emotion that combines feelings of dishonour, unworthiness and embarrassment.

"Shame you didn't get that promotion, John."

Again, is it a shame or is it regrettable, unlucky? If this word is one of your frequent words, by saying "shame" you are consistently reinforcing a negative emotion. You are subliminally emphasising the message to your subconscious that perhaps you are ashamed of yourself, or of something in your past, and are not quite good enough.

CASE STUDY

This brings to mind John, in his mid-60s, who had worked all his life for an insurance company. An intelligent man, he felt he had never reached his full potential. He suffered from chronic shyness and considerably lacked confidence in his own abilities. His parents had divorced when he was seven, and as a consequence he was packed off to live with his elderly grandparents, and then sent to boarding school. He was bitter and resentful towards his father, whom he felt had abandoned him, "running off with the secretary". Distraught at the break-up of her marriage, his mother took to drink, became an alcoholic and brought men from pubs and clubs back to sleep with her.

I quickly noticed he frequently applied the expression "it's a shame", or "that's a shame", inappropriately to quite inconsequential things. During one of our therapy sessions, whilst doing a regression, he expressed how ashamed he had been of his parents' behaviour, and kept it well hidden from his classmates. His friends were never invited back to stay with his grandparents in the holidays.

Part of the therapy involved him, under hypnosis, allowing his younger self to forgive his parents, and allow the hurt, shame and anger to go. We also looked at cleaning up his vocabulary to eradicate the overuse of the word "shame". By the end of our work together, he told me how he felt he could confidently hold his head up; he felt lighter and cleaner, and no longer ashamed of his past.

Try

Remember, our subconscious responds to actions, colourful words, words that are directive. Our subconscious interprets the word "try" as a woolly word, a bit of a get-out clause, it is not a definite.

Which of the following two statements makes you feel more focused to take action?

> *"I will try to finish that report and have it on your desk for next Monday."*

Or

> *"I will finish that report and have it on your desk for next Monday."*

Singer
Beverley Knight
sings, "Shoulda
woulda coulda'
are the last
words
of a fool"!

In the first statement, by using the word "try" our subconscious thinks,

> *"Okay I'll attempt it, have a stab at it. I haven't fully committed*
> *myself to anything though, phew!"*

Need

As human beings we have just a few essential basic needs: to be fed, watered, sheltered, and to feel physically and mentally safe.

Again, when we frequently include the word "need" into our everyday language we are reinforcing that we come from a place of lack. That, perhaps, something is missing, we are not complete. It is a non-progressive word, it is disempowering to our subconscious and gives a strong message to ourselves and to others that we are needy, lacking, wanting.

"Need" suggests an unconscious fear; fear, perhaps of the unknown or the unanticipated. Frequently, need is used instead of the more juicy word "desire". "Desire" suggests an impassioned verve for life. Claude Bristol, author of the bestselling book *The Magic of Believing*, wrote:

> *"It is desire for something new, something different, something*
> *that is going to change your life, that causes you to make an*
> *extra effort; and it is the power of believing that alone sets in*
> *motion those inner forces by which you add what I call*
> *PLUS-VALUES to your life. So you begin with desire if you*
> *ever hope to achieve anything ... It is the prime motivating*
> *force in all of us and, without an all-consuming desire, nothing*
> *can be achieved or gained."*

Bearing in mind our subconscious responds instantly to emotion, the word "desire" is a far more emotive, inspiring word to our Subby than "need".

Listen to these common statements:

>"I need to talk to you."

>"I need you to love me."

>"I need more money in the bank before I can take on more staff."

>"I need you to be my right-hand man."

By eradicating the word "need", you come from a place of choice to take responsibility for yourself. I suggest the following alternatives to the above needy statements:

>*"I am keen to talk to you. When would it be convenient to meet or speak on the phone?"*

>*"I love you."* ...End of story. You are unable to make someone love you – they either do or they don't.

>*"I choose to take on more staff."* That strong motivating statement sends out a strong declaration to others and to yourself that you are working towards taking on more staff.

>*"You are my right-hand man."* Why wait?

Should, Would, Could

These three words sit together. They leave Should-Would-Could people with a feeling of not quite getting it right, of not feeling in control.

"Should" is defined in the dictionary as "have to", "must", "ought".
When you say the word "should" out loud how does it make you feel?
"Should" instils what a teacher or a person of authority tells us to do, not what we want to do.

Exchange it for:

> *"Have you considered looking at another alternative?"* rather than *"You should look for another alternative."*

> Replacing "should" with "considered" feels so much more empowering. How does it make you feel?

"Would" is defined as intending or hoping for something. The word "would" indicates lack of action, someone who is indecisive.

> *"Would you like to take me up on my offer?"*

I invite you to replace this with:

> *"Take me up on my offer."*

This sounds more like you really mean it, that you have a firm intention.

Also, replace

>*"I wouldn't if I were you."*

with

>*"Have you considered …?"*

Forget

How many of you remember to re-use your plastic bags when you go shopping?

A couple of years ago the Tesco poster campaign for recycling plastic bags was:

>*"Don't forget your plastic bags."*

At the time I felt this was inappropriate wording; our subconscious just sees the words **forget** and **plastic bags** … and "Bingo!", that's exactly what many of us did on a frequent basis; I rarely remembered to take my plastic bags with me when I went shopping.

How much more effective their subsequent campaign was, which simply asked us to remember to re-use our plastic bags! So replace "forget" with "remember".

Hope

"Hope" is an interesting word. I use the word hope carefully. For some people, it comes from a place of expectation, dreams, desires. For example:

"I am hoping to visit my uncle in Australia next year."

In this example I prefer to replace "hope" with "intention":

"I am intending to go to Australia next year to visit my uncle."

The word "intention" sends a stronger message to the subconscious that you are determined, set on going to Australia, kick starting the planning, putting into place how and when the specifics of the trip. Hope feels like a long distant dream, wishful thinking with no firm action in place.

Here are some much-used phrases:

"I hope you are well."

"I hope you have a happy birthday."

"I hope you have a safe journey."

"I hope you get my cheque in the post."

What exactly are we hoping? In these contexts it conveys a feeling of uncertainty, a sense of being out of control. Change these to:

"I trust you are well."

"I trust you have a happy birthday."

"I trust you have a safe journey."

"I trust you will pay your outstanding fee."

The word "trust" sums up a feeling of reliability and confidence.

Hate

I would like to see the use of the word "hate" banished forever. It is a strong word that evokes unpleasant destructive feelings. The dictionary defines "hate" as having a feeling of intense hostility for someone or something. It is part of what I refer to as the Soap Opera Culture that has dominated our televisions for so long, reinforcing a hate and blame culture: "I hate that person", "I hate you, Tracey."

To come from a place of hate taints our minds; it is so much more preferable to come from a place of love. When we eradicate hate from our minds and our vocabulary the world feels like a safer, peaceful place. Without hate in the world there will be less space for wars or terrorism. Using hate so casually implies the concept is buried somewhere inside you.

People use the word "hate" too loosely:

> *"I hate spaghetti."*

> *"I hate my new schedule."*

In this case I urge you to replace with "dislike" or "unhappy with":

> *"I dislike spaghetti."*

> *"I am unhappy with my new schedule."*

Afraid

How many times do you hear phrases similar to these?

"I am afraid that Mr Brown is at lunch right now."

or

"I'm afraid I can't come tomorrow."

What exactly are you afraid of?

The dictionary definition of "afraid" is frightened, fearful, apprehensive, terrified, anxious, scared, troubled. We give our power away when we say "afraid" … unless we are scared of the dark, or terrified of heights.

But

"But" is a huge little word that can destroy your confidence in three letters:

"I love you, but …"

It undoes everything said previously. Again:

"Fantastic report, Jennifer … but it was late."

The "but" quickly takes away that all-essential feel-good factor, and acts as a brick wall against establishing an easy rapport with someone. Swap it for:

"Fantastic report, Jennifer! Well done! When you meet the deadline next time it will be perfect!"

Power Sap Words

A small yet significant incident has stayed with me, and is relevant to share with you here. Back in the 1980s when I lived in East London, a mother and her young son were just ahead of me on the pavement. The mother was walking ahead whilst the boy was slowly dragging behind, absorbed in his activity of running a stick along the railings of St. Marks Church, creating a wonderful clattering noise. His mother turned round, shouting at him, "Are you deaf as well as stupid? Stop doing that and hurry up!" I often wonder what that little boy's self-image is like now …

Stupid

Lots of people use the word "stupid" on a frequent basis. I am astounded at how many people constantly call themselves "stupid". It is a common throwaway remark. We say:

> *"I am so stupid."*

> *"How can I be such a stupid idiot?"*

We use it as a term of frustration or anger when we forget something or do something wrong. When we call ourselves "stupid" we are sending a direct message to our subconscious that we are silly, lacking everything on as a given. It doesn't think we don't really mean that.

The knock-on effect is that, when we continually reinforce to our Subby that we are stupid, it keeps us stuck in that behaviour. We continue to reinforce certain patterns of behaviour that continues a perpetual cycle. We continue to do stupid things.

Many years ago, before I learnt to talk to myself in a positive encouraging way, I would continually call myself "stupid" for locking my keys in the car, which was a repeat pattern for me. It was a time when I had small children and I was flustered and feeling rather out of control, juggling many things. Each time I would call myself stupid and even hit my head in a frustrated fashion. Interestingly, I no longer have this habit since I learnt to talk to my Subby in a calm reassuring manner.

Terrible

Have you noticed how we often use words out of context? How "terrible" is the fact that buses always come in threes? How terrible was your day, really? These are inappropriate uses of the word "terrible", which actually means to frighten, to terrorise, and is formidable and horrifying.

Dreadful

Another word frequently used inappropriately is "dreadful":

> *"I can't go out like this; my hair looks dreadful."*

Something "dreadful" is extremely unpleasant, shocking and frightening, like the sinking of the *Titanic*, for instance.

Lazy

"Lazy" means slothful or indolent. "Lazy" can be good to use, for example, if you want to have a wonderful lazy day basking in the garden enjoying the sunshine reading, eating and drinking.

In other contexts it creates a negative feeling: your mother or teacher may have continually reminded you that you are a lazy good for nothing. In this case, "lazy" may well evoke negative feelings, rather than powering you up to be more active.

No Problem

"No problem," said the young waiter as he showed us to our table.

"No problem," said the waiter as he brought our drinks over to us.

"No problem," said the waiter as he took our food order.

"No problem," said the waiter when I asked for some mustard.

By now I'm thinking, so what is the problem? All I can hear is the reinforcement of the word "problem"! "No problem" is a counter-productive phrase; it's okay to say it once, but to repeat it counteracts the sentiment. The impression the waiter conveyed was a lack of confidence and made us feel nervous. What was going on behind the scenes in the kitchen? Was the chef having a nervous breakdown? Had the waiter had a row with his girlfriend?

In contrast, a week later during lunch with a friend a sweet waitress replied to our thanks by smiling and saying "It's a pleasure" when she brought us our food. Just that simple phrase made me feel relaxed, reassured and pleased to be in capable hands.

Not So Bad

How frequently are you met with the following response, when asking someone how they are?

"Not so bad" or "Mustn't grumble"

Or perhaps you respond like that yourself.

Think about what you are hearing or saying. First, it gives a mixed response, so how exactly are you – are you feeling good or bad? It is not a definite answer, and it saps your power. I meet several people every day who reply with the same response. Recently I have been involved in selling my house and buying a new property. I have found estate agents are particularly prone to this "not so bad" response. Imagine how many times they are reinforcing that they are not good; in fact, they are bad. It leaves the customer with a limiting impression of the individual – can this person or organisation deliver for me? Are they up to the job? It is important to remember how the dendrites in our brains release cortisone every time we hear or repeat a negative Power Sap Word.

Quite, Might and Maybe

You either like something or you dislike it, so saying "quite" diminishes what you are saying:

"I quite like this."

Be definite:

"I like this."

Or even:

"I really like this."

And, similarly:

"I might have a go at joining a choir."

Again, be more definite:

"I am considering joining a choir."

or

"I am going to join a choir."

How often do you catch yourself saying "maybe"?

"Maybe I'll run the marathon this May."

or

"I am going to run the marathon this year."

Which statement do you think is more likely to help you get past that finishing line?

When we receive a Christmas card or other communication from someone who says, *"Maybe we can catch up next year,"* how seriously do we take them? It is a throw away comment.

Rather than "maybe" replace with:

> *"Let's put a date in the diary and meet up next year."*

The above statement is a further reinforcement to your subconscious and to others that you are authentic, dependable and have genuine intent.

EXERCISE: Mirror, Mirror, On the Wall ...
Looking in a mirror, repeat the phrase "Not so bad". Notice how the corners of your mouth turn down, notice your expression, tone and how saying those words makes you feel.

Now repeat "I'm well, thank you. Again, notice how your mouth invariably turns up into a smile and how that makes you feel lighter and more upbeat, and releases the feel-good chemical serotonin.

Can't, Don't, Mustn't, Shan't, Shouldn't, Won't

Words like this are negative disempowering words. Try this out ... what's your initial gut response to the following questions?

"I don't suppose you can do me a favour?"

"Can you do me a favour, please?"

Response to the first question is immediately "no", whereas with the second question we are more likely to think twice about what that favour is.

Here are some more Power Sap Words that elicit disempowering feelings. Take note of how these words make you feel when you hear them.

battle, blame, blocked, bored, careful, cheat, confused, could, crazy, crime, delinquent, difficult, dirty, disappointment, disaster, disliked, dissatisfied, dumb, dunce, effort, embarrass, empty, evil, explain, failure, fear, fool, foolish, forgetful, ghastly, grotesque, hard, harm, heinous, helpless, hideous, hopeless, horrible, idiot, impatience, inferior, insensitive, invalid, jealousy, lack, lacking, lame, lazy, lonely, loser, lose, loser, lost, mad, make, malevolent, mean, must, naughty, obsessive, ought, poor, problem, queer, repellent, ridiculous, sad, silly, smelly, stupidity, temper, too, ugly, unkempt, untidy, vulnerable, want, wrong.

EXERCISE: Cutting Out the Power Cut and Power Sap Words

This quick exercise will give you more practice in replacing Power Sapping Words with Power Up Words. First, look at these before-and-after examples:

> *Because I don't show my feelings it doesn't mean I don't have any.*
>
> *→ I rarely show my feelings; trust me, I have some.*
>
> *Just because I don't say much doesn't mean I haven't anything to say.*
>
> *→ I may be quiet; when I have something to say I say it.*

Next, rewrite the following sentences in your own, positive interpretation, being clear and concise:

> *Just because I'm not like you it doesn't mean I'm weird.*
>
> *Don't forget to bring your notes with you.*
>
> *I can't help feeling you don't like me much.*

In Step Four you have learned:

- **the destructive negative impact of using Power Cut Words**

- **the weakening negative impact of using Power Sap Words**

Points to Focus On

- Start to replace your Power Cut and Power Sap Words with empowering Power Up Words that make you feel good about yourself.

- Record your telephone conversations; start to listen to your common words and phrases. Are they limiting words? Identify at least six Power Cut and Power Sap Words and tell your nearest and dearest and your colleagues to pick you up on these if you use them.

Step Five:

How to Say No, and Other Power Building Scenarios

How to Say No, and Other Power Building Scenarios

In Step Five you will

- **learn how to feel comfortable in saying and meaning "no"**

- **explore how you can build up your self-respect**

- **find out how to delegate to others**

- **discover how to increase your inner confidence and keep your power**

Do you say "yes" all the time and either instantly regret it or realise somewhere along the way you have done it again? Do you end up feeling frazzled, put upon, worn out, have little time for yourself, not living your truth, and still dreaming about achieving your dreams?

Many of us are brought up with our elders constantly telling us "no" to everything, which leaves a child feeling frustrated and disempowered.

In Step Five, I want to share with you the essential art of being able to say "no" without actually saying "no", and keeping a sense of inner calm and confidence, and above all your power. You will learn how to put into practice the liberating skill of turning down a request while leaving both yourself and the other person feeling good.

This is a subject close to my heart. For years I would jump in and say "yes" to something, only to realise fairly quickly that actually I had just let myself in for something I really didn't want to do, and then kick myself for having done so. I would then spend a long time ruminating and working out how I could get out of whatever it was I had said "yes" to. Or, worse, actually having to carry out a favour or a job that took up my time and gave me no pleasure whatsoever. So why did I have a need to do that? And what was it that enabled me to stop?

Coming from a Place of Inner Confidence

Let us explore exactly what it is that prevents you from saying "no", and how to move away from repeated patterns of saying "yes" to every request. You will develop the confidence to make more informed beneficial choices for yourself, and feel in control of all aspects of your life.

Saying "yes" in certain circumstances is fine, if what you are saying "yes" to is exactly what you want to be doing … and it feels okay and sits with you comfortably. How often does that happen for you?

So let me ask you, do you pride yourself on being the kind of person everyone can rely on, always there to fix things, write that last minute report, organise an event, give a presentation and so on? Do you see your role in life to make it alright for everybody else?

Think about it… is this ability of not being able to say "no" a deep-seated desire to want to make it alright for everybody else, because of the fear of confrontation, of what might result if you were to say "no"? Or is it a repeat pattern stemming from your childhood? Perhaps you have inherited this behaviour from your parents? Or is it perhaps an excuse to prevent you from getting on with the important stuff in your life?

Or, even, have you become an expert at saying "yes" to delay discovering what it is that's preventing you from achieving your bigger goals in life? Are you an artist, a writer? Do you come up with one hundred and one reasons why you are unable to organise that art exhibition or finish writing that book? Are you too busy running around after everyone else? Or is it that you just don't know how to say "no"?

Essentially, saying "no" is all about keeping your power. It is about keeping in sight what it is that's important to you.

In today's uncertain financial climate, the pressure of work and life stress is on the increase. People are feeling more and more under pressure to prove their worth, to hang on to their jobs, to create more sales, to be more prolific in their output. I work with more and more people who feel they are stressed and not in control, and find it harder and harder to say "no".

In a work setting, saying "yes" instead of "no" can often stem from a lack of confidence, not feeling quite good enough to refuse. So you agree to deliver the goods, whatever the consequences to your work, personal and family commitments, and regardless of the fact that you are putting yourself under more pressure.

CASE STUDY

Steve is a client I worked with who came to me because he felt exhausted, burnt out and felt his life held no purpose. All his life he had prided himself on doing the right thing; if anything needed doing, he was right up there volunteering and saying "yes" to everyone's requests.

When he first came to me he had been promoted from within his company eight months previously. Instead of taking the helm of the ship and demonstrating his leadership qualities, he was still running around carrying out not only his new workload but also his old job. I quickly saw he had an inability to delegate and empower the rest of his team. He was in fact running himself into the ground, swamped, overwhelmed, not sleeping and fast burning himself out.

He still had to develop his confidence to step back and delegate to the rest of the team. Also his new line manager saw he was a soft touch and kept piling on more and more work for him to do. He just hadn't the skills and the confidence to say "no" to every request. He was worried he would lose his job; in fact, he thought he didn't even deserve the promotion.

After delving a little deeper, we established he came from a troubled background. His father was a weak-mannered man who worked long hours running the family grocery business. His mother suffered from depression and was an alcoholic with a fiery temper, so Steve and his two brothers had learnt that in order to make life easier and avoid being hit they would toe the line, overcompensating because they believed they were responsible for their mother's drinking and depression. Furthermore, he also told me that he was bullied at school, he was always being told off for coming in late, and because he was under pressure at home he hadn't the confidence or the skills to stand up for himself.

Through our sessions he learnt how to feel happier, and more confident in himself, and he began to enjoy his new promotion, learning to delegate to his team and gaining respect from his boss and work colleagues.

He discovered how to say "no" with confidence; he became a master of diplomacy, leaving behind his limiting behaviour of taking everything on to prove to himself he was some super one-man show.

Coming Up with a Compromise

The golden rule to saying "no" with confidence and to mean it is to be able to know that, whatever the circumstances, whatever the outcome, you are okay; to have a self-belief in yourself, in your decisions and your actions; to know that actually you have a choice. When and only when you respect yourself will other people respect you too. Remember, "like attracts like".

Three key stages towards respecting yourself:

Stage One: **Stop worrying about what other people think of you … start listening to yourself.** Where does it feel uncomfortable in your body when you agree to something that doesn't feel quite right? Does it stick in your throat? Do you feel it in your gut? Do you carry tension in your shoulders? Once you start to recognise and listen to your body's symptoms and what they are telling you – that it does not feel right to say "yes" – it will be easier to say "no" and feel secure in the knowledge it's okay to do so.

Stage Two: **Learn to value yourself and appreciate your own special unique qualities.** We all have our own unique DNA, and no two fingerprints are the same – we are supposed to be different. By appreciating this basic information, you can begin to take control and have the confidence to decide what it is you choose … or choose not … to do. (Go back and read the Find and Live Your Authentic Self exercise in Step Two.)

Stage Three: **Learning to be assertive and to have your voice heard.** I don't mean being aggressive and shouting, I mean listening to what YOU really want and consistently and respectfully sticking to your decision.

When I was sixteen I learnt one of my earliest and most precious lessons from my Uncle Bob whilst on holiday in Jersey, and it was the liberating art of being able to say "no". He said to me, "If you aren't sure, Nicola, when somebody asks you to do something, instead of jumping in with a 'yes' and then living to regret that decision, just say, 'the idea doesn't appeal to me' or 'I will give it some thought, and get back to you in a day or so'. ...Avoid saying 'maybe', because it gives people false hope, and they will continue to ask you until they get a definite answer."

This useful piece of information has given me time to avoid being put on the spot. It has served to ease me in to having the confidence to go from a "yes" to a "no". It will give you time to work out what it is you really want to do or don't want to do. Having the ability to say "no" can help you to grow personally as well as gain a greater respect from others.

TECHNIQUE: The Look, Listen, Learn Approach

As human beings, we are designed to be highly intuitive. Your manager, boss, client or whoever can sniff out a vulnerable, insecure person, not just by what you look like but also by how you dress, stand, your body language and the words you use … they can smell the fear they can instil in a vulnerable person. Here's how they do it.

Look

Notice and observe the characteristics of a vulnerable, under-confident person. Compare these to a confident strong individual. Be aware of how they carry themselves. What's their body language like? Do they have their arms and legs crossed in a defensive fashion or do they have a confident stance? Do they look people in the eye or look away? Are their hand gestures open and confident or constrained? Are they rocking back and forth or do they stand with their feet squarely on the ground?

Listen

Be an observer. Start to pay attention to other people. See how they respond when asked to produce an extra piece of work at short notice, or to drop everything and go and pick up the boss's dry cleaning. What kind of tone is used? Is their tone aggressive, respectful or apologetic? Do they raise their voice? Do they speak calmly, confidently? Is their tone high pitched, squeaky or does it finish each sentence on a low? Do they sound depressed or do they inspire a feeling of confidence, of someone in control?

Learn

Begin to move your observations forward and be aware of how you sound, look and behave to others. Play around with changing your tone, body language and the words you use. Ask for feedback from others. Be aware of what feels the most comfortable for you. (For more on this, work through the following Feedback exercise.)

When saying "no", be aware of the overuse of "sorry", or "I am afraid" ... those words instantly put you in a position of weakness. Rather, use words that make you feel more confident and instil a feeling of being in control. Remember, keep your power! We covered this in depth in Step Four.

There are some great books on the market about body language and how to present yourself. Several examples are included in More Information at the end of this book.

EXERCISE: Feedback

One: Observation

Observe others; take note of their tone, words and body language.

What is it about them that reassures you?
What is it that makes you feel uncomfortable?

Two: Listen

Record yourself on the telephone.

Video yourself talking to a friend.

Listen to the words you use. Be aware of your:

- tone

- words

- body language.

Three: Get honest feedback

Ask someone you know and trust to tell you where you give your power away.

Which characteristics in your words, voice, and/or body language make them feel reassured about you?

Four: Take Action

Begin to act on changing those aspects about you that give your power away.

Coming from a Place of Understanding

Next time you are asked to put more demands on your precious time – when you are confronted by a pushy, aggressive manager, customer or client – apply the simple strategies put forward in this section.

By nature I jump in; I'm an enthusiast sometimes without thinking of the consequences. By applying certain techniques I have given myself time to think and saved myself a lot of unnecessary angst and extra unwanted work.

I always aim to understand where the other person is coming from. Do they believe you are the best person for the job, a soft touch, a walk over, or can't they think of anyone else to ask?

The key thing to prevent previous patterns of always saying "yes" … is to:

- Stay calm, be aware of your breathing, keep it steady … and slow it down if your pulse is racing.

- Keep your tone and your body language open and give yourself time to think.

- If at first you are not sure what to say, I always recommend thanking them for asking you; then you might ask them to clarify exactly what they want you to do.

- If you are still not feeling confident enough to say "no", say something like … "I will give it my consideration. I will sleep on it and get back to you tomorrow/in a day or so." (Be specific as to when you are coming back to them, and ensure you do so.)

So, for example, if you are asked to deliver a report within a very tight deadline, or to give a presentation on a subject you may not know much about, a useful and effective response is:

"Thank you for asking me. I would love to help you out; regretfully I am unable to, as I have a full schedule and would want to give it my best. It deserves somebody's full attention."

Or put in a proviso or a condition; you can always meet them halfway if it suits your time framework … you can always say something like:

"I can help you out. I can give it two hours of my time next week."

The ideal is to be perceived as someone who is in control, helpful, knowledgeable and willing to help, so this is where you suggest someone else or indicate how else the request could be achieved. I always find this to be a useful response:

"Thank you for asking me, but I am not the right person to deliver that piece of work. However, have you thought about asking Melissa? I know she is looking to develop her skills in that area."

You come across as polite, helpful and honest.

If the person asking you the request has in the past intimidated you, it is essential you keep your response short; look them in the eye and be firm but at the same time respectful, neither aggressive or rude. Stick to your intention, and refrain from getting involved in a lengthy discussion. Be aware of keeping your power, rather than giving it away, and be mindful of getting twisted in knots. If it upsets them that you are unable to help, well that's their stuff to deal with, rather than yours. The more you practise and put these techniques into action, the easier it becomes.

To help you with this, refer back to SODA (in Step Three) and the four easy stages to keeping your power.

S – stop
O – observe
D – detach
A – take action when ready

The Power of Mental Rehearsal

The connection between image and the imagination is very powerful. You can harness this by mentally rehearsing saying "no" and turning it into a positive scenario. Practise this Mental Rehearsal technique.

TECHNIQUE: Visualisation

Identify something you know you have struggled with in the past –
perhaps telling a difficult client you can no longer work with them, or
informing your boss you are unable to work late every night this week.
You may like to visualise in your mind certain scenarios with your boss
or whoever you've experienced difficulties with in the past.

Work out want you want to say, and write it down so you feel
comfortable with what you want to say.

I just love this technique; it is like a preview of how the situation will
and does run.

Top sports men and women, politicians and leaders use the power of their
subconscious mind to mentally rehearse a winning result. It is what is referred
to as "being in the zone". They mentally rehearse the desired outcome by
powering up their emotions and visualising the scene.

Take it further in the next exercise.

EXERCISE: Power Rehearsal

Close your eyes and imagine you see yourself on a large screen. Take note of every detail. Notice what you are wearing, how you are standing, sitting, smiling, how confident you look, how at ease you look.

See yourself standing or sitting tall, with your back straight, and see yourself looking and feeling confident. See how you look them in the eye, how you are in control of the situation, how easily your confident response flows off your tongue. Start to feel excited about all the possibilities of being in control of your responses and your answers.

Flesh out the details of the proposed scenario. With an imaginary remote control in your hand, you can control the fast-forward button. Press play and see the scenario unfold. You can press the rewind button until you get it just right, until you have the scene in your mind.

Now turn up the colours with your remote control and when you have the perfect scene you can float into the body on the screen. Be aware of how you feel – calm, composed, and wonderfully in control – and now take three deep anchoring breaths.

- On the first deep anchoring breath ... feel the feeling of deep mental calmness flood your entire system from the top of your head all the way down to the tips of your toes and fingers.

- On the second deep breath ... anchor that powerful feeling of being physically relaxed – feel how in control you are.

- On the third deep breath ... anchor that feeling and sense it flood your entire system with competence, confidence and control.

Rehearse, Rehearse, Rehearse

Like all good actors, rehearse, rehearse, rehearse until you get the perfect performance. By acquiring and practising these skills and techniques to develop your inner confidence, you have the ability to recognise what it is you do want to do ... you are justified in refraining from making it alright for others, from saying "yes"; it will feel much more comfortable and easier the more you practise it. In fact it will become second nature.

Take time out to think clearly about what is being asked of you. This gives you more time to find the appropriate response you feel comfortable with.

The Changing Process

Frequently, when people first start to change, to value themselves more, to gain an inner confidence, not jumping in to make it alright for those around them, they can be accused of being arrogant or selfish. My response to this is that friends, colleagues, family and associates who have grown used to your old behaviour are sometimes resistant to you moving on. It is inconvenient to them; they liked it that you always said "yes" – it made their lives easier. Once you are more comfortable with looking after your own needs first, you will find you can choose to give when you truly want to, with pleasure, rather than resentfully draining your own resources.

Follow Your Gut Response

Intuitive decision making goes far beyond using common sense, because it involves additional sensors to perceive and become aware of the information from outside external factors. Sometimes it is referred to as our gut feeling, sixth sense, inner sense, or instinct. In our busy, busy, ever-increasing fast-paced lives, we frequently override our intuition.

Here I urge you to listen to your intuition; start to listen to your gut response. Just stick with it, go with your intuition. Ask yourself, who am I making it alright for … me or them? These people will eventually respect and like you for having the confidence to follow your gut response, your natural intuition. The real bonus of this is that once you learn to stand your ground – and follow your true response – you will begin to attract more like-minded respectful people to you, providing you with satisfying business and personal relationships in your life.

Remember … it's all about staying in control, developing your inner confidence, and listening to what your body tells you, what response feels comfortable to you.

By feeling more confident with yourself, you will learn to recognise it is okay … and you are okay … it is all about having your feet firmly on the ground.

Lao Tzu (ancient Chinese philosopher) said:

"The power of intuitive understanding will protect you from harm until the end of your days."

In Step Five you have learned:

- **how to feel comfortable in saying and meaning "no"**

- **how to respect yourself**

- **how to delegate to others**

- **how to increase your inner confidence and keep your power**

- **why listening to your intuition is good for you**

Points to Focus On

Practise finding alternatives to saying "no" to what you now consider to be unreasonable requests.

Apply the positive scenario visualisation technique. It changes our expectations for success – it's just like daydreaming with a purpose. Visualise someone listening to you; mentally rehearse delegating a task, and refusing to do something you don't want to do. See them listening to you and then you listening to them.

Practise SODA (refer to Step Three).

Step Six:

How to Create a Great Lasting Impression

How to Create a Great Lasting Impression

In Step Six you will

- **improve your leadership and credibility**

- **look at how the relevance of words and phrases determines how you are perceived by others**

- **change your words to change your impact**

- **look at how the power of your voice is congruent to the words you use**

- **explore why silence is golden**

- **learn how to release your negative emotions**

It is a well-known fact, isn't it, that first impressions count. We make up our minds about people within the first two minutes or less.

Therefore, it is crucial that your words, whether in the written or spoken form, have the maximum impact. People rarely remember more than a third of what we say; it is the impression, the feeling we invoke in people, that counts.

In today's business world, to be an effective leader, to enjoy a positive reputation, people want to believe in you, to trust you, to see you as credible and knowledgeable. They look to respect your opinion; they benefit from feeling inspired, led and focused.

Take a moment now to consider how often you come away from a talk or a meeting feeling inspired, powered up to take action. How memorable was that event and what was it you most remember? As we discussed in Step Three, it is mostly the feeling we retain. Again, the words we use play a vital role in juicing up our subconscious, keeping in mind that it loves and responds to metaphor and imagery. The subconscious only responds to what has been spoken; it is incapable of differentiating between what we say and what we really *mean*.

Back in the 1960s, psychologist Professor Albert Mehrabian established that a mere 7% of the message related to feelings and attitudes in the words you speak whereas 38% of the message is paralinguistic (meaning the way your words are said, for example, by the look on your face or by the sound of your voice), and a staggering 55% of the message is in your facial expression.

You could therefore ask, "So why concern myself with words?" In this book I have set out the amazing case for using appropriate words to evoke the impression, image and expectations of a successful confident person. You are trustworthy, in control, reliable and a strong leader who motivates and inspires colleagues, management and clients alike; you can represent your business or company with authenticity.

CASE STUDY

I was asked to do some work with a dysfunctional team. The recently appointed director, Ken, was struggling to make his mark. The previous director had been a bully and a tyrant who had led her team with an iron rod. As a result, long-term sickness and stress-related absenteeism had become the norm.

Team meetings were non-productive and predicted targets were way off course. Ken had been promoted from within the team and was facing a tough challenge to bring about new changes. His main tasks were to improve low morale, achieve predicted targets and get long-term sickness under control.

I began by attending a team meeting scheduled to last all day. The meeting kicked off with Ken addressing the team and went something along these lines.

"Good morning. Right, you've all received the agenda I pulled together yesterday. Hope you've had time to look at it, and as you can see we've got a packed agenda and a lot to do in a short amount of time.

Now once again our targets are very poor. We need to be getting out there and selling our message. We should try to work more effectively as a team; otherwise I am telling you heads will roll. There will be losses; you are all sitting here by the skin of your teeth. You're not paid to waste my or the company's time, I hope you understand. Am I making myself loud and clear?

What I want us to kick off with is to come up with a new strategy of how we can try and recover our reputation in the market place, win over and convince new customers to buy our products and services.

Now if you can manage to get your lazy good for nothing selves into some form of a team I want us to work together and do some brainstorming and try and come up with some new ideas. Do you think you could manage that? It would be good, wouldn't it?"

And so that set the tone for the rest of the day; the meeting rolled on very, very slowly.

What particularly amazed me was when I asked Ken how he felt it had gone, he said "Well, they know where they stand, they know I'm not a pushover, they understand I mean business. As you can see they are a talentless bunch."

I had three key things to highlight.

First, we looked at his language – he was using largely negative disempowering words, limiting words including: *should, try, need, lazy, losses, convince, not, waste, hope, would, could.*

The impact of those words, which were typical and predominant in Ken's vocabulary, worked on two levels. First, he was putting across the message that he was coming from a place of lack. As a leader, his team picked up on his limiting language, which was predominantly threatening, bullish and aggressive, and suggested he was lacking control, rather than in control. His language reinforced his lack of leadership, which this particular team was thirsty for.

Second, rather than firing up the team his language had quite the opposite effect. The dendrites (see Step One) within the team members' subconscious minds were busy firing on all cylinders, releasing masses of cortisone, aiding a spiralling down into a dark, dark hole instead of releasing feel-good serotonin which would boost the inspiration and creativity the team were craving.

Thirdly, we looked at how he continued to disempower the team in feeling stuck.

Ken and I did some fundamental work on:

- Changing his words – he quickly understood the principles of using inspirational emotive language.

- Reviewing his team on an individual basis – he quickly came to the conclusion that individually they had talents and skills that were currently underutilised.

- Preparing a realistic, tangible time-bound agenda, to be sent out four days before the meeting, with contributions from the team. Team members would take it in turns to chair the meeting and compile the agenda – he realised individuals were capable of taking responsibility.

Working with the team to help their creativity and solution-finding processes, coaching them to apply positive empowering language in their day-to-day work – he learned he could pass on what he had discovered to his team members.

All of the above were put into place over the next three months, resulting in a significant upturn in team morale. Through changing his words, Ken started to be perceived as a strong, consistent leader. By changing their words to be more dynamic, empowering and open the team began to build trust between one other. On the plus side in the long term, their financial figures began to rise steadily, and the problem of long-term sickness also lessened.

In the previous example we saw how Ken was initially a bully and a weak leader; his behaviour may have rung a bell with you. I have worked with many clients who at some time in their lives have been bullied, or consistently put down at school or work, or in some other instance.

The following exercise is an opportunity to address and reframe previous experiences of being made to feel small, or that our opinions do not count. When we hold on to this sort of damaging experience it can limit us and prevent us from moving on. Remember our subconscious holds on to emotional experiences. We can tell ourselves on a rational level it doesn't matter and just move on; however, emotive experiences stay locked within us, waiting to be released.

EXERCISE: Free Yourself

I frequently use this exercise in therapy sessions to help clients release negative emotions.

This simple and effective reframing exercise allows you to release negative emotions through a genuine and sincere forgiveness process. The process can release fear, anger, resentment, inadequacy and past hurts. When we hold on to deep-seated resentments, the only person it really impacts on is ourselves. They just get in the way and holds us back from being our true and best selves.

Make yourself comfortable, turn off phones and find half an hour just for you.

1. Close your eyes.

2. Relax your body and focus on your breathing.

3. Float all the way up in the air and to an unknown remote location (the top of a mountain, a remote beach, etc. – this is good as it enables us to be away from places perhaps "anchored" to – associated with – negative experiences).

4. Imagine sitting on a chair in an empty theatre in front of an empty stage.

5. Invite on that stage, group by group, your friends, family, colleagues, teachers, masters, partners and all the people you have met in your life (who you remember, of course).

6. Ask them all (group by group): "Do you support me, where I am going and my ambitions?"

7. Keep those who answered "no" on the stage.

8. Truly and sincerely, choose to forgive them now on the principle that you now know that everyone is doing the best they can with what they have and that forgiving will enable you to feel free. This will provide you with all the positive associated advantages; wish them good things.

9. "Cut" all the connections with everyone (including those who said "yes") and reconnect only to those you want to reconnect to in a brand new, empowered way.

10. Come back to now.

11. Open your eyes.

You will be amazed at the sense of freedom this process allows you to experience.

* I would like to thank the inspirational Luca Senatore from East Anglia Hypnotherapy for introducing me to this technique and for generously allowing me to share it with you.

Continue to Power Up Your Voice

We have already established that people make instant decisions about us and the words we use are just a small part. We have "four means of expression" when we communicate with others:

- Our words

- Our facial expression

- Our body language

- Our voice

In order for our listener to believe we are genuine, all four must give off the same authentic message.

In this section, we look at how we make people feel by the sound of our voice and indeed how our voice, along with our words, reinforces how we feel about ourselves.

Preparation

First, here are a couple of great techniques to help you become a more relaxed speaker. Practise these whenever you can.

In the words of Bananarama:

"It's not what you say, it's the way that you say it!"

TECHNIQUE: Breathing

Relax those vocal chords. Practise breathing into your stomach and see how long you can hold your breath for: 40+ seconds is good. Aim for longer breaths each time. Push the air up from your stomach, and speak from there rather than from your throat. By learning to breathe properly you are learning to project your voice. When we speak from the throat it tightens, restricting your range.

TECHNIQUE: Tongue Twisters

You can learn to relax your vocal chords by humming and yawning to stretch the muscles, or saying tongue twisters. Here is a fun one. Repeat several times:

"Peggy Babcock stood on the balcony inexplicably mimicking him hiccupping and amicably welcoming him in."

Volume

Are you softly spoken or are you larger than life with a booming voice? There is nothing more irritating than someone who speaks so softly you just can't hear them. The impression you can portray is someone lacking in confidence, who just wants to disappear and slide out of sight under the table. By speaking too softly, you run the risk of disengaging your listeners.

If you are naturally softly spoken, learn to project your voice, and practise turning up the volume.

TECHNIQUE: Speaking Over Music

Have some fun and practise speaking to the rhythm of Beethoven's 1812 Overture – play it for real or imagine it. Practise getting your voice heard over the crashing of the cymbals and other instruments. Try it out – it works!

I recommend working with a voice coach, a great long-term investment to help enhance your confidence in everyday life, in the boardroom and with public speaking.

You can also develop your speaking skills by joining the international organisation Toastmasters. Personally, I have found it a beneficial, fun way to boost confidence and learn to speak with more authority. There are lots of groups across the country.

Deliberately speaking softly can also be interpreted as a control strategy, so people have to lean into you and listen extra carefully. Equally, someone with a booming voice is also a turn off. You can be perceived as bombastic and overbearing, and written off before you have a chance to prove yourself. Aim for musicality in your voice (see later), by which I mean varying the tone and the volume.

Intonation and Pitch

In her book *How to Be Brilliant at Public Speaking*, Sarah Lloyd-Hughes describes three common categories of intonation and pitch:

- **Robot voice** – we have all sat through a meeting with someone who has no variation or pitch in their tone. By the end they send everyone to sleep or heading for the nearest gas oven. (Think of Stephen Hawking's automated voice.) Avoid droning and be aware of how other people respond to you: are they interacting, following you, or are they nodding off?

- **Dog talker** – Some people speak with a high, excited intonation and pitch, either too high or too contrasting. They are just too exhausting to be around for long. (Think of Woody Allen.)

- **Storyteller** – An engaging storyteller varies tone and intonation, and adds variety, resulting in a delightful musicality. (Think of Joanna Lumley.)

Back in the time of our cavemen ancestors or, more recently, at school, where we gathered round to hear someone relate a story, we couldn't get enough and hung on to every word. Aim to be the best possible storyteller you can be with the following techniques.

EXERCISE: Experiment with Intonation and Pitch

Stage One

Read a random paragraph from this book out loud in your normal voice. On the second read-through, start to speak and then drop your voice a little lower, adding expectation for the listener and incorporate short pauses; then come back in again with more energy and louder volume. This variety adds interest just like a storyteller. Remember, we are all natural storytellers. The more awareness you place on this, the more naturally your musicality will flow.

Stage Two

Experiment with saying "Good Morning" in an energetic upbeat tone. Then go for the flat or monotone "good morning". (You can say this to yourself, or practise on the neighbours!) Again notice how it makes you feel. The musicality – or lack of it – in your voice affects how you feel about yourself and others. An upbeat tone releases the serotonin and dopamine hormones (as discussed in Stage One); likewise, when someone has a flat or strangulated tone of voice, this sends a message to the brain, which releases cortisone, keeping you and your audience in a flat, depressed and uninspired frame of mind.

Where's your Energy?

Does your voice have energy and vigour? People pick up on the musicality in your voice. If you lead with a bright, upbeat, calm and well-paced voice, people follow the note and respond likewise. In the same way, if you are flat, monotone and drone on, you affect your listeners, who tap into the emotion and respond in the same way. And remember, it is the emotion that people remember about you.

EXERCISE: Listening to Voices

Part One

When listening to the radio, television or an enthusiastic person, notice moments of enthusiasm in their voices. How does this make you feel?

Part Two

Practise talking about something that really lights your fire. Record yourself and listen to how excited and enthusiastic you sound. You can record your voice on your mobile phone – have fun with this! Be aware of the musicality in your voice. Practise varying your tone and bringing even more musicality to your voice. Play around with how you can get more energy into your voice. Notice how others react to you when you use more varied tones and musicality.

In your own speech, it is good to strike a balance of energy to avoid sounding plain exhausting, over enthusiastic, or too slow and lethargic.

When you feel good about yourself, you will have confidence and a self-belief. Throughout this book I refer to authenticity and living your truth. The more you are comfortable with and accept yourself, the more you can be who you really are.

TECHNIQUE: Inflecting

Ron Aldridge, actor, theatre director and voice coach, teaches international businessmen and women how to use the major key.

There are three inflections we use at the end of a line.

1. Downward inflection – goes down at the end of the line.

2. Straight through the line – keeps an even tone.

3. Upward inflection – finishes the sentence by going up at the end of the line.

Newsreaders have been trained to speak in the major key, which means they speak positively with an upward inflection at the end of the sentence, or straight through the line, going neither up nor down.

Ron says, "At all times you must keep channels of communication open. Concentration and discipline with inflections will ensure this. Give importance to the final word in every sentence. Practise every day so this technique becomes normal for you and feels natural and acceptable to your ear."

Clarity

Avoid repeating the words "actually" and "basically", and steer away from clichés like "as a matter of fact", "this point in time" and "to be honest". Do these words add value or just clutter up your language?

Pace and Pauses

Again, be an observer of how professionals on the radio and television pace their conversation. How do they make you feel if they gallop along – does it make you feel calm or stressed? Take note of how Joanna Lumley speaks; she always makes me feel wonderfully calm when I hear her in an interview, as do the delightful rich tones of Desert Island Discs presenter Kirsty Young. How do Jeremy Paxman or Brian Redhead make you feel? They make me feel rushed and rather rubbed up the wrong way.

When we speak we don't have to rush along, without pausing. Pauses and silences can be therapeutic and extremely powerful for the listener. Notice how people listen to you. Are they nodding in agreement or are they looking uncomfortable and confused? Always be aware of others' body language and maintain eye contact with everyone you speak to. Pauses are good when you are speaking – next, we look at why silence is golden.

"Silence is golden,
but my eyes
still see."

– *The Tremolos*

And yes, it's okay to have a dialect. It's you, it's who you are; just take into account the above and be proud of your accent. Remember, the more authentic you are, the more confident you feel and the more plausible you are perceived as by others.

Why Silence is Golden – the bits in between the words

The gaps in our words are just as important as the words themselves. The essence of empowering silence is that it enables us to think, to take stock before we rush in with an apology, or a throwaway remark, or volunteer to do something. Culturally, as a nation we are generally disconcerted by silence, and we often feel the need to jump in to fill the void, simply to avoid what can feel like an uncomfortable quietness.

EXERCISE: The Power of Silence

Notice pauses in conversations you have with others. How uncomfortable are you with silence? Are you actually listening to the other person or people? Or are you busy thinking about the next sentence and how to respond? Also, notice how other people make you feel when they listen to you, without interruption. But do you feel wrong-footed or disarmed if they remain silent after you have spoken?

Some people use silence as a manipulative tool, to keep you in your place, and it can be threatening. Once you are aware of this approach, it is easier to deal with. The desired aim here is to be in control rather than be controlling, to have the silence in the right context. A good example is when you wish to complain, perhaps about the service of something that has been inadequate. After you have expressed your point, and without giving your power away, in a reasonable, assertive manner and with a level tone, ask an open question:

"I trust you see my point of view....What can you do for me... How can you help me?"

Then leave a wonderful empowering silence … let the other person respond. Just keep quiet for as long as it takes for that other person to respond. You have given them an open question, just as in a game of tennis, to come back with a return, in their own time. (Facial gestures are important too – look at them with sincerity in your eyes and face.)

Aim to be aware of letting the other person have the last word. Don't give your power away – agree to differ in your opinion. Or just let the other person have the final goodbye; we often needlessly keep a conversation going because we don't know how to end it and put the phone down or walk away.

Why is silence in conversation beneficial?

- It gives gravitas to your message; pausing mid-sentence keeps the listener engaged and gives them time to absorb what you are saying.

- It provides a space for you to gather your thoughts.

- It is an opportunity for the listener to show respect for the speaker.

- It is a space for listeners to reflect before they respond.

- It is an opportunity to show feelings by responses (e.g. body language like a smile or a nod) where words are inadequate.

Grace, serenity and gravitas accompany a person who effectively applies silence in their everyday toolbox. Such an individual feels and projects a strong, confident presence; we feel reassured, valued and heard by someone who listens to us.

In Step Six you have learned:

- **to use positive language to improve your leadership and credibility**

- **how the relevance of words and phrases determines how others perceive you**

- **how to release negative emotions to power your change**

- **how to further develop your confidence and your authenticity**

- **how the power of your voice is congruent to the words you use**

- **why silence is golden**

Points to Focus On

- Pay attention to other people's voices, with the following checklist noting:

  how they make you feel

  pace and pauses

  their clarity and musicality

  tone and dialect

- Practise the art of golden silence and notice how you are responded to.

- Do the Releasing Negative Emotions exercise earlier in this Step.

Step Seven:

Seduce Yourself and Your Listener with Your Powerful Message

Seduce Yourself and Your Listener with Your Powerful Message

In Step Seven you will:

- **learn how to write copy that juices up your subconscious**

- **discover how to sell your message**

- **identify powerful words that light up your vocabulary**

- **learn how to speak with authority and passion, to be seen as a motivated, inspired person**

Power Up your Subby to evoke fantastic feelings and actions.

How to Write Powerful Copy that Juices Up Your Subconscious

EXERCISE: Your Juicy Words

Which words make you feel good?

Which words give you positive feelings?

Which words make you feel comfortable, stimulated and motivated?

Make a list of the words that appeal to you. Your aim here is to get your confident message across to yourself and to others.

As well as the verbal language you use in emails, correspondence, report writing, strategies etc., aim for words that are strong, progressive and inspiring. Re-read your emails, letters or documents several times, and read them out loud, before sending them. Ask yourself, "How does this make me feel?"

Our diverse and beautiful language has many words and images that encourage us to feel comfortable, at ease and happy. Naturally we are all different, and some words appeal and will work more effectively than others.

When writing powerful copy, the key thing to remember is to use words that make you feel:

- excited and motivated

- confident and secure

- sincere and honest, building rapport

- clear in your intentions.

Double-check exactly what feelings you are conveying. Are you giving away your power? How confident are you in your message, and how confident do others feel about you and the service you provide?

Powerful Words that Light Up Your Vocabulary

Here are some categories of words that help to Power Up your Subby to evoke fantastic feelings and actions.

"Words that enlighten the soul are more precious than jewels."

Hazrat Inayat Khan

Energetic and Motivating Words and Phrases

Focus, focused, forward thinking, forward approach, gifted, inspirational, brilliant, inspired, inspirational, cleverly, passion, powerful, dynamic, zest, enthusiastic, succeed, success, successful, exuberant, stimulating, endorse, fervent, creative, easily, strong, effective, effortlessly, desirable, vibrant, progressive, opportunity, empower, progressively.

Trust-invoking Words

Forgive, gentle, gift, harmony, assured, honest, investment, intelligent, kindness, knowledgeable, naturally, calmly, can, manage, perspective, confident, peacefully, perfectly, profoundly, process, connected, safely, acceptance, remember, respectful, receive, trust, protected, responsible.

Feel-good Warm Words

Good, healthy, happy, happiness, harmony, balanced, joyful, blessing, loved, loving, nurture, comfortable, comforting, peaceful, relaxed, delicious, contented, soft, affluent, appreciate, tenderly, well, healthy, warmth, settled, rich, quick, easy, enjoyable.

EXERCISE: Words that Power Up Your Subby

How many words of your own can you add to each of the previous three categories? You can create your own categories too.

Here's a useful example of words chosen to instil confidence:

> "Welcome aboard and thank you for flying with Supersonic Airways. We look forward to ensuring we deliver to you a first class service. It is our pleasure to make your journey comfortable and enjoyable. For your safety please remember to refrain from using any electronic equipment during take-off until we inform you it is safe to do so. We trust you have an enjoyable flight. Feel free to just sit back and relax and enjoy your flight."

As opposed to:

> "Thank you for flying with Supersonic Airways. We hope you have an enjoyable flight. Please don't forget to turn off your mobile phone or any other electronic equipment until we tell you to. We are here to make sure you have a trouble-free flight. Just ask, no problem is too big or too small."

The first statement makes us feel safe and secure – they use words like "welcome", "trust", "ensuring", "first class", "pleasure", "safety", "comfortable", "remember", "enjoyable". All these words instil confidence in a passenger. In contrast, the second statement flags up to our subconscious feelings of insecurity: "hope", "forget", "trouble", "problem", "no", "big", "small", "don't".

Consider the following text from a holiday tour company. This does an effective job at leaving the reader with a feeling of being seduced by the

The Sensatori Experience

"Sensatori holidays have been designed to fuel your senses. After all, our enjoyment is based around touch, taste, smell, sight and sound. The more senses stirred, the more we enjoy the experience – and never more so than when we're on holiday. But appealing to the senses is only half of the concept. We also turned to the idea of 'satori' – a sudden feeling of enlightenment. And so that's how the word Sensatori came about. It's that split second when everything just comes together. So how does Sensatori become a reality? The answer is simple – experiences. That could mean volleyball on the sands first thing in the morning. An aroma stone massage late afternoon. A candlelit dinner al fresco. Or it could just mean lazing by the pool with the sun on your face.

The key to it all is balance. That's why Sensatori brings you so much choice. You can just pick and mix the bits that suit you, whether that's action-packed sports or relaxing spa treatments."

language; the lasting impression is of a wonderful, life-enhancing treat.

The above is a fantastic example of how we are seduced by the deliciousness of words. As we read this we are right there on that holiday, or booking it up before you can say "Indiana Jones"!

Email Example

Here is a perfect illustration of an email sent to me by a client cancelling one of our early therapy sessions. Sasha, a highly intelligent and vulnerable woman, was just coming out of a messy and emotional divorce. Her ex-husband, a tyrant and a bully, had, over time, totally eroded her confidence. Sasha's work with me was to rediscover herself, to enjoy being a single woman again, and to pursue her desire to train as an accountant. I include her email here because it perfectly demonstrates the power of our words and how they can keep us locked in our limiting behaviour.

> *Dear Nicola,*
>
> *I have had some difficulties lately and have to rearrange so much stuff. I have to therefore humbly ask for our appointment to be cancelled for tomorrow and I will be in touch later on in the week to try to allocate another time. I am very sorry about this and hope to speak soon.*
>
> *Best wishes*
>
> *Sasha*

The Power Sap and Power Cut Words, in bold, are clearly keeping her in an unfortunate place of inferiority and victim mode. Here is my response, with Power Up Words (in bold) to reinforce to Sasha that she can choose to be liberated from her burden:

> *Dear Sasha,*
>
> *First, happy to rearrange, thank you for letting me know.*
>
> *Second, you have used humbly and sorry and try … all these words reinforce that you are coming from a place of lack.*
>
> *Remember you are not a walking apology; you are instead*

a wonderful, strong, intelligent woman, who keeps her power rather than giving it away to other people. Those words reinforce your past.

Sorry = sorrow

You are not humble!

Try is not a definite

Best wishes

Nicola

Here is a suggested alternative email from Sasha, which is far more agreeable:

Dear Nicola,

Trust you are well. I am writing to rearrange my next session with you, giving you 24 hours' notice as requested. I look forward to my next session and will phone you in due course. I have a lot going on in my life just now, hence prioritising my time.

Thank you for your understanding.

Best wishes

Sasha

Short, sweet, to the point, and I am clear about her intentions.

EXERCISE: Be Exciting!

Go back to a report or an important document that you or someone else has written. On a scale of 1–10, grade it for how excited it makes you feel. Does it excite, motivate, and inspire you confidently to take action towards achieving the desired goal or outcome? Or do the words feel heavy, flat, or uninspiring as you read them? Take a moment to note your reactions. In its current format, how do you think it will inspire and create a dynamic impression?

Now, go through and change the language to make it more powerful and compelling. You can use a different coloured pen, or different font colour if you do this on screen. Really have fun with this exercise; give it your all, to Power Up the message you intend to convey.

After editing the text, notice how much more motivated it leaves you feeling. Ask the opinion of someone else.

EXERCISE: Your Power Up Document

Now we come to the real fun. How would it be to write a document so powerful that, every time you read it, it makes you feel good, excited and continually reinforces that feel-good feeling?

Back in 2002, studying to become a hypnotherapist and NLP practitioner, my life was rather fast paced and stressful, as I had also just taken up a promotion. I really felt I was in the fast lane, learning lots of new things, and managing staff, concepts and procedures. I used the skills I was learning with my hypnosis course to write myself what is termed an empowering hypnotic suggestion; here we will call it a Power Up Document.

It worked like a dream, and helped to resolve my feeling of being out of control, overstretched and potentially losing the plot.

I want to share with you the three easy steps to writing your own Power Up Document. Before you begin, remember the golden rules we have studied throughout the book:

- You get what you ask for – through the Law of Sympathetic Resonance, or the Law of Attraction.

- Using powerful dynamic Power Up language fires up your mental energy, releasing the all-essential feel-good chemical serotonin.

- You can change the way you feel about something by seducing your subconscious with juicy, motivating and comfortable words.

Phase One

Write down what it is you want to change. So, for example, my list of what I wanted to change was:

- To stop feeling overwhelmed by emails, meetings, and report writing

- To stop wasting my time

- To sleep better, to stop feeling tired

- To stop skipping lunch, or eating rubbish

- To stop thinking about work at the end of the day

Phase Two

On a separate piece of paper, write down what you do want (i.e. the desired end result). My list was to:

- feel calm

- feel in control

- relax with friends and family at the end of the day

- achieve a good sense of balance in my working day

- be efficient with my time

- enjoy beneficial relationships at work

- feel more energetic

- take time for a nutritious lunch

Phase Three

Create your own mind map, or whatever works for you.

Phase Four

Then have a play. Using your list of your personal favourite Power Up Words (see the Words that Power Up Your Subby exercise, earlier in this Stage), write your own Power Up Document. Use the present tense to give a sense of immediacy.

Here is an excerpt of the Power Up Document I wrote all those years ago:

> *After waking up refreshed after a deep and wonderfully refreshing night's sleep, I benefit from enjoyable, productive working days. My first initial waking thoughts are calm, happy, pleasing ones that fill me with joy and pleasure.*
>
> *I take delight in rewarding and beneficial working relationships. Working together with colleagues and meeting people connected with work, my relationships are more fulfilling, fun, richer. My increased mental calmness and confidence creates warm, respectful relationships with other people.*
>
> *I am more and more wonderfully calm, which contributes to my increased feeling of being naturally fluent, self-assured and creative, inspiring and enjoying new challenges and welcoming new learning experiences as my self-belief grows stronger and stronger.*

"Pleasant words are as a honeycomb, sweet to the mind and healing to the body."

Proverbs 16:24

I enjoy this good feeling of being more skilled at planning my time. Increasingly more focused on keeping on track, with my eye on my goals. Careful to maximise my outcomes by carefully monitoring how much energy I put into each project and role.

Just the exercise itself of planning, reviewing and rewriting what I did want, and focusing on it, made a dramatic improvement to my working day. Applied to hypnosis techniques too, it works even more quickly. If you want to know how to apply self-hypnosis to Power Up your life even more effectively, you can find out how you can work with me in More Information at the end of this book.

In Step Seven you have learned:

- **how to write text that juices up your subconscious**

- **how to sell your message, whether it's an email, a letter, a company report, or a one-minute pitch**

- **powerful words that light up your vocabulary**

- **how to speak with authority and passion, to be seen as a motivated, inspired authentic person**

Points to Focus On

- Repeat the Be Exciting! exercise, rewriting an existing report.

- Create your own unique personal Power Up Document to help reinforce your goals.

Conclusion

This is the end of the book, *Mind Your Language: Seven Steps to Success through Word Power* and just the beginning for you. If you have worked through the simple exercises you will already be benefiting from what you have learned and are putting into practice. If you have just read through the book, to really help reinforce your experience I recommend you go back and work through the exercises and practise the easy and effective techniques.

As you begin to use more positive language in your daily life, you will notice yourself becoming more and more empowered. The benefits from this are many. You will:

- attract others to you

- be less stressed

- experience success

- be energised physically

- be more upright in your posture

- be a better leader of others

- have a better memory

- cope better with difficult situations

- be happier

- be more confident and in control

- be more creative

- inspire more trust

- develop greater rapport with others

- be taken more seriously

- be more dynamic and productive

- achieve your goals and start setting more

In a nutshell, choosing and using Power Up Words on a regular basis means you will no longer be stuck in a self-reinforcing cycle of negativity. Axing Power Sap and Power Cut Words from your vocabulary preserves your personal energy so you are no longer negating everything you say. Just notice how you are now listened to and believed, by others and also by your own mind – you will start to believe in yourself, enjoying more confidence, rapport and trust in every area of your life.

P.S. You may find, in time, that you slip back again. Feelings of doubt, insecurity and fear are all part of the human condition, and can sometimes creep back into our lives during specific life events. If this happens to you take some time and review what your current behaviour and responses are. You will probably find that you have stopped applying some of the fundamental stages that I have outlined in the book. This is simply remedied; just refer back to the book for extra reinforcement to remind yourself of the stages.

Good luck and have fun as you benefit from the results.

More Information

My contact details

Email:nicola@nicolamenage.co.uk

Web:www.nicolamenage.co.uk

Blog:www.nicolamenage.wordpress.com

Twitter:#Nicolamenagehyp

Facebook: http://www.facebook.com/pages/Nicola-Menage-Hypnotherapy/

Acknowledgements

I give grateful thanks to all the clients I have worked with, a number of whom I have used as case studies. To honour their privacy all identities have been changed. My appreciation also goes to a few key mentors and authors who have all greatly added to my knowledge and experience. Special thanks to Lizzie Quartermaine and Alison Thompson for applying their editing skills and shaping this book into order.

Bibliography

Most of these books were in my head and my heart as I was writing this book. I have also included a few extra resources you may find useful.

Body Language for Dummies, Elizabeth Kuhnke, Wiley, 2007

Feel the Fear and Do It Anyway, Susan Jeffers, Vermilion, 2007

Finding Meaning in the Second Half of Life: How to Finally, Really Grow Up, James Hollis, Gotham, 2005 (first published 1963)

Goal Mapping: The Practical Workbook – How to Turn Your Dreams into Realities, Brian Mayne, Watkins Publishing, 2006

How to be Brilliant at Public Speaking: Any Audience, Any Situation, Sarah Lloyd-Hughes, 2011, Pearson Life

Body Language: How to Read Others' Thoughts by Their Gestures, Allan Pease, Camel Publishing, 2001

Instant Confidence (book and CD), Paul McKenna, Bantam Press, 2006

The Magic of Believing, Claude M. Bristol, Frontal Lobe Publishing, 2011

Messages from Water: Vol. 2. World's First Pictures of Frozen Water Crystals, Masaru Emoto, Hado Kyoikusha, 2004

The Power of Now: A Guide to Spiritual Enlightenment, Eckhart Tolle, New World Library, 2004

Quantum Healing: Exploring the Frontiers of Mind/Body Medicine, Deepak Chopra, Bantam, 1989

Super Brain: Unleash the Power of your Mind, Deepak Chopra, Rudolph E. Tanzi, Rider 2012

What to Say When You Talk to Yourself: Powerful New Techniques to Programme Your Potential for Success!, Shad Helmstetter, Harper Collins, 1991

You Can Heal Your Life, Louise L. Hay, Hay House Publishers, 2004

About the author

As a motivational hypnotherapist, Nicola helps people increase their self-belief and self determination, enabling them to making lasting changes in their lives.

She uses hypnosis and other mind programming techniques to put people from all walks of life back in control of their own future calmly, safely and quickly. Describing her work she says *"I excite the subconscious to see benefit and create fundamental change, so life is easier, happier and healthier."*

Nicola brings her very own sense of fun, passion and energy to a range of motivational speaking and seminar engagements—all with an insightful and pertinent message. She uses her diverse experience of life and work to make each session powerful and compelling.

Her journey has led her from being a student of fine and decorative arts to developing teams within a large public sector organisation, from the vibrancy of London to the rural tranquillity of the Cotswolds – not to mention the varied learning experiences of setting up and running her own private hypnotherapy practice.

Nicola also works with companies and organisations of all sizes delivering individual and team programmes on motivation, leadership and progressive team development.

She has two daughters now grown up and flown the nest. Nicola lives and works in Oxfordshire.